I0647439

R G MENZIES ESSAY

FIT FOR SERVICE

MEETING THE DEMAND
OF THE ASIAN MIDDLE CLASS

ANDREW BRAGG

MENZIES
RESEARCH CENTRE

connorcourt
PUBLISHING

Menzies Research Centre
January, 2017

Series Editor: Nick Cater

Published in 2017 by Connor Court Publishing Pty Ltd

Connor Court Publishing Pty Ltd
PO Box 7257
Redland Bay QLD 4165
sales@connorcourt.com
www.connorcourt.com

Phone 0497 900 685

ISBN: 978-1-925501-37-7

Cover design, Ian James

Printed in Australia

Japan is a country with which we were recently at war, and whose conduct of the war was such as to produce immeasurable bitterness among our own people. But we are now at peace. Are we to say that we will not trade with Japan?

-- Robert Menzies

What is the duty of the Government? Is it to please the affected local manufacturer and sacrifice a substantial share of our wool market, or is it to preserve our export markets in the interest of the entire nation?

-- Robert Menzies

Any advantage, favour, privilege or immunity which has been or may hereafter be granted by the Government of either country to any product originating in or destined for any third country shall be accorded immediately and unconditionally to the like product originating in or destined for the other country.

-- Australia-Japan Commerce Agreement

Those developing countries which over the last 50 years that have practised open trading, have practised open policies towards foreign investment, that have put their faith in a more free market approach, those have done best.

-- John Howard

A nation that would enrich itself by foreign trade is certainly most likely to do so when its neighbours are all rich, industrious, and commercial nations.

-- Adam Smith

Table of Contents

FOREWORD

Turning Trade Commitments into Commercial Success

Opening Australia to the world during the past 35 years has served our nation well. We are in our 25th year of recession-free growth, averaging 3.3 per cent annually. However, the massive build-up of government debt in recent years by major developed world countries has stymied growth and rendered impotent the major fiscal and monetary policy levers.

As the Coalition came into government in 2013, it was clear a new policy focus with a much greater attention on trade and investment to drive growth and jobs was needed.

The government set its sights on completing free trade agreements with South Korea, Japan and China in its first term of office.

Within two years, quality agreements with the three countries – two of which former Prime Minister John Howard had begun almost a decade earlier – were finalised. Tariffs have been lowered dramatically or removed totally. Concessions on access for so many Australian services have been granted, with China granting concessions not given to any other country.

So for the first time we are starting to see many small and medium-sized Australian service providers exporting their services in health, pharmaceuticals, aged care, education, water management, engineering, IT, architecture, construction, agricultural services, tourism, resources and energy, design and much more.

As Minister for Trade and Investment from 2013-2016, I regularly talked about services being the next wave of Australian exports.

Many of the concessions provide Australia with an extraordinary platform; but it is just that, a platform. For Australia to make the most of the agreements, we need to take the initiative, engage with prospective trade and investment partners and explore the opportunities in these markets of more than 1.6 billion people.

This publication for the Menzies Research Centre, an institution of which I have been a director since 1994, focuses on turning these hard-won commitments into exports and ultimately Australian jobs. The Menzies Research Centre and its Executive Director Nick Cater should be congratulated for commissioning this research as a forward-looking policy project.

History will record that the 44th Parliament passed broad-based trade deals with three of Australia's four largest trading partners in North Asia. I trust the 45th Parliament will continue building on this legacy by enhancing our competitiveness, concluding trade agreements with all major trading partners and implementing these with zeal.

As well as we have done in trade policy in recent years, we can always ask is there anything we can do better? It is timely that this contribution assesses whether our institutions can deliver the trade policy capacity Australia needs, reviews our approach to services trade and urges us to put competitiveness at the centre of domestic policymaking.

The Hon Andrew Robb AO

INTRODUCTION

Learning from history to provide the services of tomorrow to Asia

Australia has an ambitious trade agenda. Bilateral agreements with China, Japan and South Korea are symbolic of grand ambitions but will we capitalise on these opportunities? The gains of the last three years could easily be lost by a lack of commitment to competitiveness, a lack of interest in complex policy, a failure to respond to rapid technological change or by pandering to growing calls for protectionism. Australia cannot afford complacency. History shows that our prosperity has been based on 'institutions that provided incentives for investment, trade and innovation'.[1] We undermine those institutions at our peril.

This monograph draws out the lessons from our history and shows how much individual vision and institutional capacity shaped the evolution of Australian trade policy since World War II, which has so dramatically contributed to the high standard of living we enjoy today.

If ever there was a time to look outward, not inward, it is now.

---

[1]   James A Robinson and Daron Acemoglu, *Why Nations Fail: The Origins of Power, Prosperity and Poverty* (Crown Business, 2012), pp. 102-103.

Yet there is a growing sense in Australia of policy amnesia. We have forgotten what created the 25 year long run of economic growth. It was deregulation, liberalisation and reducing subsidies and cutting tariffs. It was putting a competitiveness lens over policy decisions and ultimately the value of free trade and open markets. We must win these arguments again.

Our history has given Australia strong institutional capacity in areas of traditional trading strength, such as mining and agriculture. But the monograph highlights our institutional weaknesses in the area of services, which now comprises 70 per cent of our economy. Our North Asian Free Trade Agreements open the door to Asia's growing middle class which is estimated to reach three billion people by 2030 but we have to move quickly to convert the exceptional commitments into actual exports.

This is no easy task. The competition is intense and technology is disrupting market dynamics in ways we could not have imagined even a decade ago. Ironically, we are closer to the centre of global economic power just as technology is reducing the importance of geographical proximity. Our competitors come not just from dynamos like Singapore but outward-looking post-Brexit Britain.

Technology has swept away the established business models of taxis, newspapers and hotels. The number of industries enjoying natural trade protection is shrinking daily. Who would have imagined five years ago that a taxi driver in Geelong would compete with an operator based in California? Nevertheless protectionism is on the rise. Global merchandise trade measured by value fell by 13 per cent from $US 19 trillion to $US16 trillion in 2015.

Australians are not an inward-looking people. Our penchant for travel, embrace of migrants and early adoption of new technologies sits oddly with a narrow, inward debate on public policy. While Singapore talks of competitiveness, Australia is fixated on fairness. We need to remember that there is nothing fair about stagnant wages or losing your job in a declining economy; the fairest thing is a choice of jobs in a buoyant economy where aspiring workers are upwardly mobile. But for the economy to be buoyant we must be internationally competitive. Unfortunately, we have allowed ourselves to tumble down the competitiveness indices; we must get back into contention for the top ten. We may be the lucky country but no one owes us a free kick.

A new approach is required if we are to be fit for service. We can no longer afford glacially slow trade deal implementation. Trade agreements need to be able to evolve to keep pace with change. The age of blockchain and bitcoin requires much closer interaction between the Department of Foreign Affairs and Trade and technology-enabled service sectors generating exports.

Trade agreements must be a point of departure not a destination, particularly in the implementation of hard-won services commitments. Drawing on my work in the inherently dynamic financial services sector, I propose a revised framework for services trade dealing with language, technology, timetables, mutual recognition, and reporting, transparency and accountability mechanisms.

To succeed we must learn from our mistakes such as the failed mutual recognition scheme for managed funds with Hong Kong and the free trade agreement committees that meet only once a year to fix a date for the next meeting.

This is an age of technological wonders but individuals matter more than ever. Australia's trade history shows that individuals can create national prosperity if governments create a competitive platform. Iron-ore magnate Lang Hancock showed what one man could achieve by opening the Pilbara. Former trade minister Andrew Robb skewered the rent seekers and red herring propagandists to quickly secure North Asian trade deals that languished for a decade. The next Lang Hancock may well be an Australian exporting agricultural, engineering or financial services. We need to make sure there are no barriers to these exports otherwise we will all be poorer.

The Government's role is to let people get on with developing ideas and commercialising them while it makes the country competitive and connected and gets out of the way. The wealth of the future, like the wealth of the past, will be created by individuals, not the state. As Menzies said, 'We have learned that true rising standards of living are the product of progressive enterprise, the acceptance of risks, the encouragement of adventure, the prospect of rewards. These are all individual matters. There is no Government department which can create these things.'[2]

We live in uncertain times. We face the threat of trade hostilities between the US and China, the US withdrawal from the Trans Pacific Partnership, its potential replacement by the Regional Comprehensive Economic Partnership which includes China, the new trade relationship with an independent post-Brexit Britain and commitments to conclude trade agreements with Indonesia and India. Our best insurance is to be as open, competitive and agile as possible. We need to build on traditional trading strengths as well as exploit our comparative advantages to provide the services of tomorrow to Asia's growing middle class. Our future prosperity depends on it.

---

[2]   Robert Menzies, *Afternoon Light*, 1967, p. 282.

1

Lessons from history

Core institutions

From wool and wheat boards, to swiftly opening trade relations with Japan after World War II, to the creation of the Cairns Group and achieving services market access commitments to China, we have been canny, innovative traders. Without the ability to sell our wares in foreign markets, Australia would not be the thirteenth largest economy in the world and Australians would not enjoy our relatively high living standards.

Exports are valued at over $300 billion and represent almost 25 per of the Australian economy as measured by Gross Domestic Product (GDP).[3] At this juncture, we cannot afford to give any ground to the protectionists. We must re-litigate the arguments which have been won in the past. The damage of protection and populism must be better known. Our history has the answers we need today.

The institutions and individuals that most influence trade policy are the Prime Minister and Trade Minister and their ministries, the Department of Foreign Affairs and Trade and industry

---

[3]   Austrade and The Australian Bureau of Statistic (ABS) – cited in Thirwell.

representatives, both groups and individuals. The capacity of these institutions is critical. As a former secretary of DFAT recently said:

> Perhaps because we inherited our public institutions rather than created them, we have not always appreciated just how important institutions are to good governance. And in turn how good governance is the foundation for the prosperity and security of a nation… We take sound institutions for granted. And yet they are the bedrock of our society.[4]

We have pools of institutional capacity in sectors of tradable strengths, such as mining and agriculture but industries of the future such as services, are not sufficiently organised to influence trade policy.

An old Australian debate: free markets vs protection

Re-litigating and again winning the arguments for free trade in a country like Australia is odd but par for the course. We are natural beneficiaries of free markets. An endowment of land for agricultural production and a broad array of mineral resources encouraged trade and foreign investment dating back to John McArthur in the early 19th century and the 1850s gold rush. As Angus Taylor wrote: 'Since Macarthur's first bale of wool left our docks and arrived in England in 1807, free access to fast growing global markets has been deeply etched in our economic history and national consciousness.'[5]

Throughout our history, a reasonably small number of products have dominated our exports (see graph on page 17).

---

[4]   Peter Varghese, DFAT Secretary's Speech to IPAA, 9 June 2016.
[5]   A. Taylor, 'Australia's economic openness under threat', *Australian Financial review* , 27 August 2015.

Unsurprisingly, wool, wheat, coal and iron ore dominate the past century as the number one export. Matters of trade and foreign investment featured heavily in the deliberations leading to the Australian federation in 1901 and have remained hotly contested ever since. NSW was a free trading colony and Victoria sought protection from foreign competition. The protectionists prevailed for most of the twentieth century.

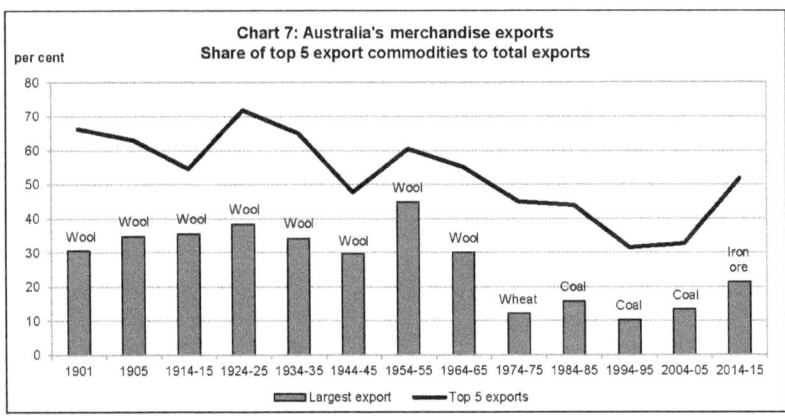

Source: Australia's merchandise exports: Frank Bingham, Australian Department of Foreign Affairs and Trade.

Protectionism hit its zenith under John McEwen, who was leader of the Country Party for 13 years in the Menzies era.[6] His signature policy was 'protection all round' which was a controversial but consistent component Australian economic policies until the 1980s.[7] 'Protection all round' involved high tariffs on manufactured goods and subsidies for Australia's primary industries. The government

---

[6]   John Howard, *The Menzies Era* (Harper Collins, 2014).

[7]   Nigel McCarthy, 'Alf Rattigan and the journalists, agenda setting in the Australian tariff debate 1963-1971', *Australian Journalism Review*, December 2000, p. 89.

protected manufacturers and supported farmers to produce.[8]

This stance was maintained as the European and North American farm subsidisation polices and development of the European common market in the 1960s damaged Australia's agricultural interests: 'Australia was particularly affected by EC (European) policies in its exports of sugar, beef and veal, grains dairy products and fruits.'[9]

McEwenism and 'protection all round' came under pressure towards the end of McEwen's career in the early 1970s from individuals such as G.A. Rattigan – the head of the Tariff Board, later Productivity Commission.[10] The war against protection was eventually won when the tariff walls were collapsed in the 1980s by the Hawke government. The arguments against free trade should be easily discredited because they are so well-known: As Prime Minister Turnbull told me:

> We have been here before, we know protection doesn't work. The US erected trade barriers in the 1920s such as through the Smoot-Hawley Act and the era of protectionism led in great part to the Great Depression. A country like Australia, we are a medium sized economy and exports are a very big part of our economy. Our trade is dominated by minerals but nonetheless, if we get into an environment where trade barriers start going up, we will really suffer. We have a massive vested interest in open markets. We should never go down the protectionist route. People who argue we should are speaking directly against the national interest.[11]

---

8   *Ibid.*
9   Don Kenyon and David Lee, 'The Struggle for Trade Liberalisation and the Cairns Group', Australian Department of Foreign Affairs and Trade, 2006, p. 18.
10   Ian W McLean, *Why Australia prospered: the shifting sources of economic growth* (Princeton, New Jersey Princeton University Press, 2013) p. 221.
11   Hon Malcolm Turnbull, interview, 2 September 2016.

Winning the essential arguments today requires a clear memory on the nation's past capacity to overturn protectionism and populism.

Menzies' Pivot to Asia

Australia started to pursue an independent trade policy after World War II. As Britain decolonised Prime Minister Robert Menzies was acutely aware of the challenges Britain's changed role in the world posed to Australia and started pivoting Australian trade focus towards Asia.

The first significant trade agreement Australia struck was with Japan on July 6, 1957 which 'gave formal expression to what has become the most enduring trade relationship that Australia has had with any country since World War II.'[12] Menzies showed tremendous vision embracing Japan just twelve years after the war had ended.

The agreement was strongly supported by farmers and greatly increased export opportunities for wool which was a primary consideration for the government. It was also vital to the growth of Australia's coal and iron ore industries. But it was bitterly opposed by manufacturers and by Labor as it gave Japanese manufacturers access to the Australian market. Labor leader Arthur Calwell even compared it with the appeasement of Nazi Germany:

> Japan's armies of 1941-45 were our enemies … they remain our enemies into the future, no matter what we may do or give … No condition, no surrender, no compromise would mean anything to the Japanese Government unless Australia … abandons the White

---

12 John Howard, 'Speech to Australia-Japan Conference', The Quay Restaurant, Sydney, 29 April 2001.

Australia policy, at least as far as the Japanese are concerned.[13]

Menzies argued:

> I have the honour to be supported in the Commonwealth
> Parliament by about 100 members. Of these, 69 are ex-members
> of the armed services. Their love of Australia is proved in action.
> Of these, no fewer than 32 served against the Japanese in the
> recent war. Of these, five were prisoners of war in Japanese hands.
> Are these members pro-Japanese? Or have they realised that the
> happiness of the future depends upon the future, and not nursing
> the bitterness of the past for cheap political gain?[14]

In 1970, Menzies' Trade Minister John McEwen said in defending the agreement he was '…taking my political life in my hands.'[15] Menzies was prepared to weather a storm of controversy because as he explained:

> There is much organisation of special interests for political
> pressure … If the Government does what they want, they are
> happy; if not, they will be hostile and bitter. Yet, no Government
> can please everybody … And a Government should not try to
> please everybody, for it ought to have principles and a mind of its
> own. The ultimate responsibility of a Government is to do what it
> thinks is best for the nation as a whole.[16]

The Japan deal delivered a win for farmers and miners against the will of the manufacturers who campaigned against the agreement. It demonstrated the benefit of organising a strong industry association to influence policy. The institutional benefit of the debate was

---

[13]   Arthur Calwell, 'That Soft Talk To Japs Is No Good!', *The Truth*, 14 February 1954, p. 9.
[14]   Robert Menzies, Radio Broadcast, 17 March 1954.
[15]   John Howard, *The Menzies Era*, (HarperCollins, 2014), p. 237.
[16]   Robert Menzies, Radio Broadcast, 16 September 1953.

that the department had to develop policy expertise in agriculture, manufacturing and later mining to brief the minister of the day on the veracity of the arguments from each side.

Before the advent of national industry groups such as the National Farmers Federation, created in 1979, most farming bodies were state-based and often had commodity-based interests. This didn't limit their ability to influence the national government. As John McEwen told a 1964 conference of producers he saw a fine line between government and farmers:

> What I did as Minister in charge of negotiations was not merely to consult this body and every other organised body in Australia but actually to take to Brussels and to London with me representatives of the organised growers or producers. If they couldn't sit at the table, they were in the room outside where I or my officials could nick out and have a word with them. This is a pretty good relationship between government and primary industry...[17]

Peter Morris of the Minerals Council of Australia argued the commercial impact of the Japanese agreement was almost immediate:

> It helped to grow Australia's coal and iron ore industries... Japanese steel mill contracts followed, including a five year, 720,000 ton contract with Corrimal and a 1.2 million ton (not tonnes) contract with Coal Cliff, both agreed in December 1958. Queensland began to export to Japan in 1961 when Thiess' Moura/Kianga mine sent 12,000 tons of coal to Japan to test its acceptability. The following year Thiess secured a contract with eight Japanese companies to

[17] John McEwen, 'Address to Annual Conference, Australian Primary Producers' Union', 21 October, 1964. Quoted in K. Campbell, 'Australian Farm Organisations and Agricultural Policy', *Australian Journal of Agricultural Economics*, 1966, p. 124.

export 2.4 million tons of coal over five years.[18]

Menzies opened markets for Australia when we most needed them especially when, in years to come our largest trading partner, Britain joined the European common market in 1973.

Farmers and free trade

The National Farmers Federation, where Robb worked as an economist in 1980 and as Executive Director from 1985 to 1988, played a major role in the development of trade policy. Robb experienced first-hand the policies of the Federation settlement were beyond repair:

> Tobacco had an effective protection rate of 400%. I walked into a
> tobacco maker and they couldn't even afford to put a floor in the
> kitchen. They were just so uncompetitive. Even with an effective
> tariff rate of 400%![19]

In 1980 the NFF published Farm Focus, co-authored by Robb and David Trebeck, a blueprint for economic reform that called for governments to control inflation, increase global competitiveness and ensure wage flexibility. It put the NFF at odds with the National Party and much of the Coalition government.

The NFF recognised that European and North American farm subsidies were damaging Australia's agricultural interests, particularly exports of sugar, beef, veal, grains, dairy products and fruits. In response, the NFF promoted trade liberalisation policies. It put the NFF at odds with its traditional ally, the National Party. As John Howard said: 'The NFF was important to our policy development

---

[18]   Peter Morris, Minerals Council of Australia, interview, 7 July 2016.
[19]   Andrew Robb, interview, 28 June 2016.

during this period. There was some disagreement within the Coalition in the 1980s over deregulation of the domestic wheat market.' Howard acknowledged the importance of Robb and former NFF president Ian McLachlan:

> They accepted the need to phase out subsidies to primary industry. Otherwise you were arguing inconsistently. They recognised the costs of tariffs are borne by our export industries, as they always had been. The NFF was strong on financial deregulation and industrial relations reform. The NFF argued strongly for an open economy and the removal of protection.[20]

The NFF emboldened the Labor Government's reform drive under Prime Minister Bob Hawke and Treasurer Paul Keating. At the opening of NFF House in 1985, Hawke said his consultations with McLachlan and his predecessor Michael Davidson had been of 'inestimable value' to the government and the rural community adding:

> We are pleased that the NFF broadly shares the Government's distrust of "solutions by regulation" as a means of solving problems.[21]

In 1985 during the Hawke government's tax summit, the NFF staged one of the largest demonstrations held in Canberra and McLachlan told a gathering of 45,000 farmers:

> We don't want to be subsidised to produce and then subsidised to export, we are not after short-term handouts. But we are sick and tired of subsidising the rest of Australia. We want the government to remove taxes on our productive inputs, we want all the taxes taken off fuel, so that we can get down to level terms

[20]   David Uren, *Takeover: Foreign Investment and the Australian Psyche*, Black Inc., 2015.
[21]   Bob Hawke, 'Speech at the opening of NFF House', Canberra, 14 May 1985.

with international competitors.[22]

The NFF did not restrict itself to a domestic mandate. It was closely involved in the establishment of the Cairns Group in 1986, a process in which Robb says the NFF and Labor Trade Minister John Dawkins were 'equal partners'. The NFF's influence earned it a hearing with US President George Bush Snr during his visit to Australia in 1992 when the NFF presented a petition of over 60,000 signatures demanding an end to US agricultural subsidies.

The 1985 rally raised $10.8 million for the court cases the NFF were running against the union movement.[23] The NFF also established a presence in Washington D.C. during the height of the subsidies debate in North America in the 1980s. Congressmen from non-farming, manufacturing states were the focus of the NFF's presence by explaining the subsidies and protection arrangements were inhibiting the capacity to export manufactured goods.[24]

The NFF provided Hawke and his Ministers the cover that helped Menzies push through the Japanese commerce agreement three decades earlier. In Robb's words: 'We became the first business group to use the media to great effect. We had people like McLachlan who were great leaders and advocates, McLachlan was the best agri-leader I ever saw.'

Mining and minerals

Spurred on by the commerce agreement with Japan, Australia's resource industry expanded steadily in the 1960s and 1970s with the opening

---

[22] Ian McLachlan, Address to National Farmers Federation rally, Old Parliament House, Canberra, 1 July 1985.

[23] Andrew Robb, interview, 28 June 2016.

[24] *Ibid.*

of the iron-ore fields of the Pilbara followed by the development of nickel, coal, and gold reserves. Bauxite, nickel, tungsten, rutile, uranium, oil and natural gas were to follow.

In November 1960, Canberra agreed to the partial lifting of an iron-ore export ban that had been in place in Australia since 1938. Its removal had been opposed by Australia's biggest miner Broken Hill Proprietary (BHP). The export ban strengthened the company's domestic steel monopoly, shielding it from foreign competition.

Thanks to individual tenacity and sound economic argument the embargo was lifted in full in 1966. In Western Australia, Lang Hancock focused on removing the pegging ban which prevented individuals and companies marking iron-ore deposits they had discovered. This was removed in Western Australia in 1961. Hancock lobbied through newspapers, books and the 'Wake up Australia' campaign of 1979 which introduced Gina Rinehart to the public.

Hancock claimed the most important literary work in his life was the Western Australian Mining Act; WA politicians such as David Brand and Charles Court supported his ambitions to develop iron ore. Hancock brought geologists to WA to participate in his famous exploratory flights, described by John McRobert as acts of extraordinary individualism: 'A superb bush pilot in a fragile, basic flying machine had done what no major company in the country had been able to achieve.'[25]

In 1967, the mining industry created its own body, the Australian Mining Industry Council (the Minerals Council of Australia from 1995). AMIC opposed protection from its inception. Its 1987 annual report recorded its extensive work with the Industries Assistance

---

[25]   John McRobert, 'Hancock Booklet'. Extract available online at: http://www. hancockprospecting.com.au/wp-content/uploads/2015/10/discovery_flight.pdf

Commission (later the Productivity Commission): 'The group's thrust has been to argue for reduced input costs to the industry through lower tariffs and reduced government support.' The 1990 annual report said 'reducing assistance to inefficient industries has been one of the major achievements of the Hawke Government. It has produced benefits for other industry sectors, including mining and the Australian economy generally.'[26]

Hancock's achievements show that self-interest and the national interest align when measures contribute to long-term economic growth. It also highlights the value of corporate and industry leadership supported by political vision. We must foster an environment where individuals can drive change to benefit the nation.

Mining leaders have often argued Australia does not have a monopoly on commodity exports just as we do not have a monopoly on good ideas. For this reason, the MCA fought the imposition of a competitiveness-sapping 'super profits' tax in 2010. Contemporary Australian mining has maintained a fine tradition of civic engagement with a heavy focus on competitiveness. As Gina Rinehart, Executive Chairman of Hancock Prospecting reminds us:

> Being internationally cost competitive is absolutely essential to our nation's economic future, and the living standards of Australians that depend upon this. Companies around our nation, particularly in the North, face challenges, added to which are very expensive and onerous government and regulatory hurdles, and compliance burdens that often our competitors and many firms in Asia, do not have to try to cope with.[27]

Australian business has struggled to deliver the trifecta required

---

26   Australian Mining Industry Council annual reports.
27   Mrs Gina Rinehart, responses received via email, 20 September 2016.

for effective policy advocacy: a credible policy agenda, supported by an evidentiary base and a sustained communication campaign which connects with the community. Too many business groups have achieved steps one and two but failed on communication. All too often we see policy papers drafted and the communication approach is an afterthought, is overly doctrinaire or preaching to the converted. All of the above sometimes applies.

But our history tells us both the NFF and MCA have connected with the broader community with grass roots advocacy. The New Zealand Initiative provides another example of a business coalition which strengthened Prime Minister John Key's hand in improving New Zealand's competitiveness through structural tax reform.

The contemporary platform: North Asian FTAs

Despite the best efforts of our institutions, multilateral trade initiatives have proven elusive. The Global Agreement on Tariffs and Trade (GATT) that evolved into the World Trade Organisation in 1994 was charged with creating a global agreement for reducing tariffs and facilitating trade. The WTO has been working on the 'Doha Round' since 2001, which broke down in 2008 and was rebooted in 2013. It is highly unlikely to yield agreement in the foreseeable future.

In the absence of multilateral trade liberalisation, the Howard Government sought a free trade agreement with China. Howard recognised the national interest was at risk if it only sought multilateral trade liberalisation; Australian exporters would be disadvantaged when competitors such as New Zealand signed bilateral deals. Negotiations commenced with China, our largest trading partner, in April 2005. With New Zealand/China negotiations already underway, Trade Minister Warren Truss focused on agriculture.

The Howard Government then opened negotiations with Japan in 2006 during Shinzo Abe's first administration following a feasibility study in 2005-06. When the Coalition lost government in 2007 neither agreement had been concluded. The Korean FTA was initiated by the Rudd Government in 2008 but Trade Minister Simon Crean said multilateral trade liberalisation was Labor's 'top priority.'[28] The Korean negotiations were blocked on two issues: Investor State Dispute Settlement (ISDS) and car tariffs but Labor was unable to finalise any of the trade agreements. Peter Hartcher wrote that Craig Emerson's April 2013 admission that Australia had 'given up' on a comprehensive trade deal with China was a 'failure'.

The three North Asian agreements were all concluded by the Abbott Government and are the broadest yet reached. Prime Minister Tony Abbott was determined to get the deals done. He said:

> I took the view the best deal was the enemy of the good. You can wait forever. I wasn't prepared to do that. If you say this is important and we have to get it done, we'll take the best deal we can get confident that what we can't get today we can get tomorrow through most favoured nation clauses and so on, well you can make things happen.[29]

28   Simon Crean, 'Australia's Role in Addressing the Future of the Multilateral Trading System', Speech at the Crawford School of Economics and Government (ANU), Canberra, 8 April 2008.
29   Hon Tony Abbott, interview, 29 June 2016.

China

The deal eliminates tariffs on dairy, beef, wine and wool by 2026 and most tariffs on resources will be removed by 2019 including almost immediate removal of tariffs on coking coal, copper, zinc, nickel and aluminium. Pharmaceuticals will be tariff free by 2019 and access is guaranteed for legal, educational, telecommunications, financial, tourism, aged and health-care services.

Japan

When Robb concluded the deal in 2014, the agreement reduced or eliminated tariffs for beef, wine, dairy and seafood by 2024 and all Australian resources, energy and manufactured goods would be tariff free by 2034. The agreement allows access to legal, financial, educational, telecommunications and a range of professional services.

Korea

To get a deal with Korea Robb says:

> I put ISDS and the removal of our car tariffs to the Koreans and we got the deal. Twelve hours later, the Japanese called. The Japanese did the best deal they've ever done. The only agreement with an agricultural nation.[30]

The Korean FTA Robb concluded removed or reduced tariffs on beef, dairy, wine and sugar. It removed tariffs on all resources over 10 years and allowed access for legal, communications and financial services.

---

[30]   Andrew Robb, interview, 28 June 2016.

Robb was able to conclude the agreements because, unlike Labor, he wasn't constrained by the unions; a realist who valued bilateral deals, with extensive knowledge of trade developed in his years leading the National Farmers' Federation and the Cattle Council of Australia, he was not distracted by the red herring Investor State Dispute Settlement. He brought genuine expertise to the parliament and ministry which benefitted all Australians.

One disadvantage of bilateral trade agreements is they tend to create extra work for export-focussed businesses – the 'noodle bowl' effect – whereas multilateral agreements reduce compliance costs. In the medium term, the North Asian FTAs may be superseded by regional agreements.

In the meantime, our North Asian FTAs deliver immediate export opportunities. As Robb said in August 2015 at the National Press Club:

> With no WTO deal in two decades, in the modern era, as a country you've got to row your own boat in cutting bilateral trade deals, or risk our economy missing coming waves of growth. Waves can be caught, or if you leave your run too late, you can miss the cut and the next set may be a long time coming.[31]

Thanks to ChAFTA, Chinese imports of bottled wine have grown by 60 per cent, lobster exports have tripled and milk powder exports have doubled.

Under the Japan FTA, Australian wine exports increased 233 per cent in 2015 (its first year of operation) compared with 2014; exports of almonds have grown twelve-fold and exports of grapes have grown ten-fold.

---

[31]   Andrew Robb, 'National Press Club Address: Trade and Investment, A Formula for Growth', National Press Club, Canberra, 12 August 2015.

In 2015, KAFTA delivered a billion dollar boost to the Australian economy. For example, exports of bottled wine increased 54 per cent in value and 43 per cent in volume when compared with 2014. Sugar volumes have doubled and liquefied natural gas has tripled with more concessions to occur in coming years.

The platform delivers quick wins in the traditional trade fields of agriculture and mining. Meanwhile we have barely scratched the surface on services implementation.

Investor State Dispute Settlement: threat to sovereignty or union dogma?

Investor State Dispute Settlement (ISDS) mechanisms were a major obstacle to the North Asian free trade agreements. ISDS is a legal framework in international agreements that allows foreign investors to take a host state to a tribunal if a treaty breach is alleged.

Labor blamed the ISDS was for its inability to reach trade agreements. 'We do not and will not support investor-state dispute settlement provisions,' Labor's former trade minister Craig Emerson declared in 2012. At the 2016 election Labor pledged to negotiate ISDS provisions out of existing agreements.

There are three points which are rarely aired on ISDS: one, it supports the rule of law as a conscious act of sovereignty. Two, Australian companies benefit from ISDS protection which is often a precondition for investment and three, the tribunals used in relevant cases are not secret.

First, a report by the Centre for Independent Studies (CIS) says ISDS mechanisms support the rule of law by reinforcing a legal framework that has been a cornerstone of free markets since the

Magna Carta. That hasn't persuaded its opponents.

The Greens cite Philip Morris's attempt to overturn plain packaging cigarette laws through the Permanent Court of Arbitration in Hong Kong even though Philip Morris lost the case. Similarly, the US has won all 13 ISDS cases brought against it in the 30 years since ISDS mechanisms have been included in trade and investment agreements. Robb describes the threat of ISDS as 'union dogma'. He says: 'We've had (them) for 30 years, we've got ISDS clauses with over 20 countries and we've won the only case brought against us.'[32]

Second, ISDS mechanisms provide legal protection for Australian investors. Australian investors recently used ISDS mechanisms in India and consistent with general practice only one of the three Australian-initiated cases were successful. Alan Oxley, a former Australian chairman of the GATT, said:

> For one of our big shopping centre businesses establishing in Chicago or Michigan, where in the United States state authorities do intervene, and I can envision a circumstance where they would erode the right in the free trade agreement for that investment to take place, then the natural response would be to use the ISDS system of arbitration to address that.[33]

Research shows a connection between ISDS mechanism or other investment treaties and levels of foreign investment. Neumayer and Spess found 'developing countries that sign more bilateral investment treaties receive more FDI inflows.' Unsurprisingly, higher investment levels are linked to a desire for legal enforceability:

---

[32] Andrew Robb, Interview, 28 June 2016.
[33] David Donaldson, 'Government-less arbitration: why trade officials like ISDS', *The Mandarin,* 11 November, 2015.

(treaties) guarantee certain standards of treatment that can be enforced via binding investor state dispute settlement outside the domestic judicial system.[34]

Asian Development Bank research fellow, Alisa DiCaprio, concludes that the ISDS clause 'is likely to promote foreign investment'.[35] Critics cite the Productivity Commission and the Chief Justice of the High Court Robert French. In its 2013-14 Trade and Assistance Review, the Productivity Commission said ISDS did not protect most Australian foreign investment because it was in the U.S, U.K and New Zealand. It also feared ISDS could expose the Commonwealth to unfunded liabilities and criticised the lack of transparency in many cases. Yet the cost of the plain packaging case – some $50 million – is not sufficient to justify blocking FTAs.

Australian investment is rapidly growing in Asian nations, some of which have very different legal systems. In 2015, Australia had $542.6 billion in foreign direct investment (FDI), more than double our $230 billion in FDI in 2001. China is Australia's 5th largest FDI destination. In 2001, our FDI in China was $395 million, just 0.002 per cent of Australian FDI. In 2014, Australia FDI in China was $14.6 billion – approximately 2.6 per cent of our total FDI. FDI in ASEAN economies has grown from 6.3 billion in 2001 to 37.6 billion in 2015, 7 per cent of Australian FDI.

Thirdly, the tribunals and processes of ISDS are alleged to be secret. Yet the plain packaging case was heard by the Permanent Court of Arbitration, which was set up by the Hague Convention, hardly a flimsy or discredited heritage. The second test of plain

---

[34] Eric Neumayer & Laura Spess, 'Do bilateral investment treaties increase foreign direct investment to developing countries?' (LSE Research Online, 2005), p 17.

[35] Alisa DiCaprio, 'Is it a problem when investors can sue the state?', Asia Regional Integration Centre, 28 May 2012.

packaging laws occurred between Uruguay and Philip Morris in July 2016, which was resolved in Uruguay's favour in the International Centre for Settlement of Investment Disputes. The Centre is part of the World Bank – an institution established following WWII and the Bretton Woods conference of 1944. The Centre itself was established in 1965 and its enabling treaty has been ratified by 151 nations.[36]

ISDS is capturing broader global attention as the Trans Pacific Partnership, which contains ISDS, goes under the microscope. To formalise the established convention that governments do not 'give away' rights under ISDS, the TPP exhaustively protects Parliamentary rights to legislate for public welfare, health, safety and enviromental reasons.[37] The last word goes to Dartmouth trade expert Douglas Irwin who wrote in *Foreign Affairs*:

> And despite populist claims to the contrary, the TPP's provisions for settling disputes between investors and governments and dealing with intellectual property rights are reasonable. In the early 1990s, similar fears about such provisions in the WTO were just as exaggerated and ultimately proved baseless.[38]

Ministers matter

Australia has done very well from its North Asian trade agreements. We have beaten Japan to China and beaten the US to Japan.   But given the statements made by Rudd/Gillard trade ministers on ISDS and multilateralism, Labor could not have concluded these agreements. ISDS provisions would also have been a stumbling block for Labor negotiating the Trans Pacific Partnership. The agreements

---

36   ICSID annual report 2015, p. 5.
37   ITS Global Report, Trans Pacific Partnership, August 2016.
38   Douglas Irwin, 'The Truth about Trade', *Foreign Affairs*, July 2016.

show an effective department was able to deliver once it had a capable minister. But the Prime Minister must select the right minister and be personally engaged as the leader of the Government. Former Prime Minister Tony Abbott said of his outlook:

> I wanted the leaders (of Japan, China and Korea) to know we didn't have tickets on ourselves. We didn't want to lecture the world; we didn't want to keep the world at arm's length. I wanted to be outgoing rather than someone who was a big headed, know-all who wanted to lay down the law. We wanted to be outgoing as a helpful friend and a trusted partner.[39]

Setting a 12-month timetable was an innovation that worked. Abbott said:

> Officials can string things out forever. By setting a timeline to get it done, we showed the Chinese, Koreans and Japanese we meant it ... I knew we needed to drive these negotiations from the top, otherwise they would linger on forever. Ultimately all politics is personal and I knew we needed to make the negotiations personal to conclude the deals. The 12-month deadline was a big part of that.[40]

Abbott and Robb's contribution to the North Asian deals is unquestionable. This is not to dismiss the work of others who negotiated for almost a decade. The better the department, the better the advice, the better the trade deals. The department needs strong institutional capacity to prioritise and advocate with counterparts. Building and maintaining its capacity is especially important when a ministry has less talent for statecraft and trade policy.

---

[39] Hon Tony Abbott, interview, 29 June 2016.
[40] *Ibid.*

Making our trade institutions fit for service

The Department of Foreign Affairs and Trade needs a much broader industry liaison program. Conventional wisdom must be turned on its head. Instead of relying on industry to provide its perspective on existing or prospective trade agreements (the 'push method'), the Department should form its assessments by getting closer to the market (the 'pull method').

This is especially true of services industries which do not have industry-wide organisations. Most services sectors and individual entrepreneurs do not engage with government. When it comes to technology, the great enabler of innovative products and services, we must look to individuals – not lumbering companies – for new ideas.

Australia rode on the sheep's back for much of the 20th century thanks to trade policies developed through the close relationship between a succession of ministers with a close interest in primary production and coordinated industry bodies that represented primary industry and developed at the end of the 19th century. The ability of the agricultural industry to pull at the nation's heartstrings and exert political pressure on MPs bolstered the development of departmental capacity.

It is unlikely history will repeat itself in the 21st century with the creation of similar industry bodies to drive trade policy across the sprawling, disconnected services and technology sectors. Recognising this institutional difference is the first step. The traditional approach to trade policy cannot be relied on when the economy is likely to be unrecognisable in 20 years. The leading ASX companies in two decades' time probably do not even exist today.[41]

41　　Nigel Andrade and Peter Munro, *Australia 2034: Luckier by Design*, (LID Publishing, 2015).

Participants in many industries will have to navigate trade agreements on their own. Yet sectors such as FinTech, AgTech and Medical Tech, which are developing new ideas daily, are not resourced to read lengthy texts which will rapidly become redundant.

The Department of Foreign Affairs and Trade needs to be much closer to the market to ensure the agreements it negotiates actually make it possible for companies to export services to Asia. DFAT needs to embed staff in dynamic industries so they understand disruptive technology and it should publish the number of staff with experience in each industry sector. Treasury opened Sydney and Melbourne offices in 2014 and 2016 to improve its understanding of financial services. The Australian Computer Society has proposed the establishment of an independent policy advisory organisation and the secondment of government officers on long-term placements to bridge the gap between private and public sector experience in the information age.

Dynamic digital agreements

Disruption means large swathes of the economy will innovate rapidly outstripping the glacial pace of government. Uber and AirBnB show regulation quickly becomes outdated. Rather than sticking to the old practices of agreeing on strange terminology in paper-based trade agreements which only boffins understand, we need to use common language that can be quickly updated in step with technological process. FTAs have 'committee' processes which sometimes review trade documents just once a year. We should convene standing meetings on implementation with permanent industry liaison in sectors experiencing rapid technological change.

H2 Ventures founder Ben Heap says: 'Governments take years to make and implement policy. Start-ups change their approach several times a day.' It is in Australia's interest to achieve 'dynamic' trade agreements. We need what Heap describes as 'rapidly iterative regulation' and rapidly iterative trade agreements.

We need to move from paper-based documents to a digital platform containing general principles for market access as well as specific undertakings where jurisdictional sensitivities preclude certain services or products being supplied by a foreign entity. We should institute this process of continuous improvement swiftly; in the corporate world it is part of many commercial contracts.

We should reduce the secrecy surrounding trade negotiations and recognise the ability of innovators such as Uber to enter foreign markets is reducing the protection afforded by regulation. The first mover advantage Australia has with China shouldn't be underestimated. We should be aiming to export the next generation of Ubers and AirBnBs under our FTA with China. This thinking should be incorporated in the FTAs we are seeking with India and Indonesia.

Trade policy must make it possible for individuals to trade Australian ideas. The ideas of one individual can boost national prosperity if properly harnessed. The next Lang Hancock may well be a person with an idea that uses today's technology to turn an idea into a service in a month. The test of institutional capacity will be whether they can turn that service into an export.

2

Servicing the Asian middle class

Services represent 70 per cent of Australia's economy but only 19 per cent of exports. They rely on intellectual capital, an infinite if universal resource. Barriers to trade in services are not tariffs but legal architecture. Abolishing tariffs is politically hard but technically easy; abolishing non-tariff barriers requires the creation of new legal frameworks.

Traditionally, most nations have focused on tariffs as a measure of trade liberalisation and have paid insufficient attention to non-tariff barriers which are critical to services. This is manifested in numerous services commitments we have entered into with no dates or deadlines and even fewer with clear mechanisms for implementing commitments. To realise commitments for services, we rely on non-tariff regulatory agreements or licensing. For example, in engineering and financial services, effective market access requires that regulators and professional bodies create a framework for mutual recognition.

FTAs create a framework for bilateral or multilateral trade but they rarely guarantee immediate market access because the standards countries use to ensure the safety of products and the qualifications of service providers can, intentionally or unintentionally, become impediments to trade.[42]

A free trade agreement negotiated between governments without direct private sector input may result in services commitments that are instantly redundant.

In an age of disruption, while national and state governments are losing control over licensing regimes for services such as hotels and taxis, the tax and legal systems largely remain state monopolies. We cannot expect disruption to deliver the right to serve the growing Asian middle class. The legal system and courts will prevent many services being provided unless there is legal access guaranteed by an FTA or equivalent. For financial, legal and engineering services a licence to practice could be granted by an FTA.

Services can be as important to Australia in the 21st century as wool and wheat were in the 19th and 20th centuries if we become a world leader in services trade policy and implementation. 2015 marked the 100th anniversary of the Australian Wheat Board but a bureaucratic services board is not the answer; we need a new framework for services and FTA implementation to ensure trade agreements genuinely benefit Australia.

Ultimately, the private sector will create the ideas and opportunities. Government's role is to remove barriers and lay the groundwork for success. But the services economy has different trade policy needs. For example, Emma Weston of Full Profile, an agricultural technology start-up, says we need national policy 'that is not about picking winners; it is about winning' whereas Andy Hutchings-Broso, chairman of Hong Kong-based Australian coding

---

[42] Inquiry into the business utilisation of Free Trade Agreements - Parliament of Australia 2015

company APIR systems, says: 'Australia's approach to exporting appears to belong to an old playbook. Provide top cover and let the market get on with it. Competing in Asia, it needs a revision as there is usually a number of strong national agendas at play … and the world is becoming hyper competitive.' We need an intelligent analysis of the support public policy settings can provide to the export of services.

Harnessing technology

There are two drivers of service export opportunities: growing wealth in the Asian region and the exportability of services through technology. The OECD predicts there will be three billion middle class Asians by 2030, around one billion in China, one billion in India and one billion in ASEAN countries and they will increasingly demand international services. While the cost of providing services is falling, the opportunities to provide services are rapidly expanding, thanks to technological developments. The Productivity Commission writes:

> Technological advances in information and communications technology (ICT), including email, online video and audio calls, and online payment systems have greatly reduced the costs of delivering a range of services and have allowed a wider range of service providers and consumers to come together. The internet allows trade in many types of services without the need for providers or consumers to be in the same physical location, avoiding travel costs.[43]

---

[43]   Productivity Commission, Inquiry into barriers to services exports 2015, p. 14.

A stocktake of service types

Australia is a relatively small exporter of services which comprise only 19 per cent of GDP, much lower than the leading service exporters such as Luxembourg (155 per cent), Ireland (53.4 per cent), Singapore (45.6 per cent) and Hong Kong (36.5 per cent).[44]

Austrade defines four types of services:

- Cross-border supply

  Services delivered from one country or territory to another. The service supplier and consumer generally do not meet. For example: a consultant in country A advises a client in country B by email, fax or phone.

- Consumption abroad

  Services delivered in one country to consumers who travel abroad, for example, as tourists, students or patients.

- Commercial presence

  Services delivered by a supplier through commercial presence in another country, for example, an insurance company establishes a branch or office in another country.

- Presence of natural persons

  Services delivered by supplier as a natural person who travels to deliver the services. This covers only temporary entry and stay of service providers, for example, an IT consultant who travels from one country to another to fulfil a contract.[45]

---

[44] *Ibid*, p. 143.
[45] Defining Services Trade – Trade in Services 2014-15, p. 155

Austrade chief economist Mark Thirlwell refers to education and tourism as 'traditional' services and the others as 'modern' services which it is now possible to export because of technological advances and trade agreements which have boosted the 'tradability' and therefore the viability of modern services.[46] Tourism and education are well-established and do not rely as much on trade agreements as modern services do.[47]

Types one, three and four are based on cross border or direct provision in a foreign country and are typically permissible if effective trade policies are in place. Provision of services using these methods in finance, law or engineering bears the closest resemblance to exporting wool and wheat a century ago. Supporting modern services trade is the most important new element. The good news is we are heading in the right direction. Export of services rose 9 per cent to $63 billion in 2014-15, increasing the proportion of services exports from 17.3 per cent in 2013-14 to 19.7 per cent in 2014-15.

Deloitte has identified five sectors where we have a comparative advantage and the potential for 'super-growth': 'agribusiness, gas, tourism, international education and wealth management.'[48] Three are services but only one is a 'modern' service. Despite these opportunities services policy lobbying is poorly organised. Services have no common agenda in the way mining and farming often share a platform. Legal, engineering and financial services have little in common with tourism or education. As Servcorp chief operating officer Marcus Moufarrige says:

> We need a thoroughly modern approach to services trade but

---

[46] Trade and Investment Note, Australia's Exports of Services: A High-Level Primer, November 2015.

[47] This is not to diminish bilateral ancillary agreements such as Air Services Agreements and visas to support education and tourism.

[48] ABS catalogue 5368

we view exporting through a 20th century prism which will not translate for services.[49]

The challenge is to develop the export potential of Australia's services. The diverse and unconventional implementation requirements need to be understood. Since many offshore markets maintain a high level of regulation, we will continue to rely on FTAs for regulatory access however, in some instances, market access can be achieved by leapfrogging regulation with technology. The example of Uber should be embraced but we should not expect offshore markets to unilaterally collapse their barriers in response to technological change.

Leapfrogging technology or finding other ways to achieve market access liberates enterprise from government but is an uncertain business model as regulation can be subsequently introduced to the exporter's detriment. Achieving market access through trade agreements and a subsequent implementation framework is usually slower but less risky. The test is whether technology-based exports can use the trade platforms of the future.

Key service exports: traditional and modern

Australia's primary services exports are a mix of traditional and modern: travel/tourism, financial, telecommunications and education services:

---

[49]   Marcus Moufarrige, interview, July 2016.

Australia's exports of services, 2015

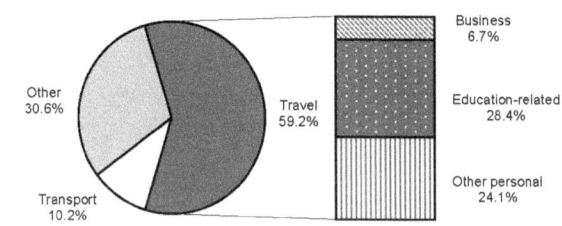

Selected other services exports by major type, 2015

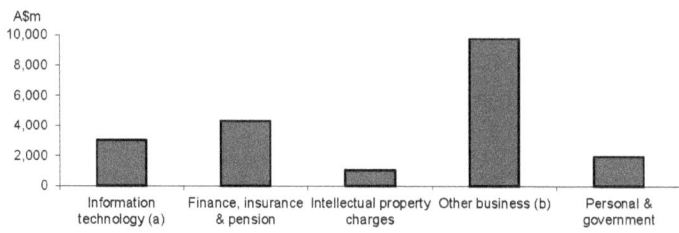

The large 'travel' component includes personal travel and our single largest services export: education. Given Australia's success in education and tourism this monograph focuses on how to increase modern services exports.

Exports of services by type of activity, 2014-15

		Value (A$ billions)	Share of total service exports (%)	Share of total exports (%)
1	Education-related personal travel	18.1	28.9	5.7
2	Personal travel ex. Education	14.6	23.3	4.6
3	Professional services & management consulting	4.8	7.7	1.5
4	Business travel	4.3	6.8	1.3
5	Financial services	3.6	5.8	1.1
6	Technical, trade related & other business services	3.4	5.4	1.1
7	Other transport services	2.7	4.3	0.8
8	Passenger transport services	2.5	4.0	0.8

9	Telecom, computer & information services	2.4	3.9	0.8
10	Postal & courier services	1.4	2.2	0.4
	Sub-total for top ten exports	57.8	92.3	18.1
	Other services	4.9	7.7	1.6
	Total exports of services	62.7	100	19.7

Source: Austrade Economics: Trade and Investment Note, p. 13.

The table highlights that the most exported modern services are professional, business and financial services. China is our number one destination taking around 20 per cent of exports. In the top five are the US, UK, New Zealand and Singapore. The next five are India, Hong Kong, Japan, Malaysia and Korea.[50] Indonesia, Vietnam and Thailand also feature in the top 20.

Australia is starting to increase modern services exports. The five-year trend growth in a traditional services exports such as inbound travel from China is 8.6 per cent, India (5.8 per cent), Japan (1.6 per cent), Korea (3.5 per cent) and Indonesia (2.8 per cent).[51]

This compares with much faster growth in modern services exports, for example financial services exports to China have grown 96.4 per cent, India (70 per cent), Japan (29.1 per cent), Korea (7.2 per cent) and Indonesia (21.1 per cent).[52] For telecommunications, computer and information technology, services exports to China have grown 7.7 per cent, India (11.5 per cent), Japan (2.9 per cent), Korea (3.3 per cent) and only Indonesia shows a reduction of 19.1 per cent.[53]

---

[50] Austrade data: top services export markets, p. 28.
[51] *Ibid*, p. 34.
[52] *Ibid*. p.38.
[53] *Ibid*, p. 42.

These figures demonstrate certain services exports can be provided without the formal legal architecture of an FTA on a cross border basis or directly in the host economy without sovereign governments lifting a finger. The growth of services exports ahead of the FTAs is striking.

Thirlwell explains:

> growth in exports of financial services and telecommunications/ information technology can largely be explained by two factors. Firstly, higher incomes drive a higher demand for services in general. Secondly, technology reduces barriers to services trade. Government is still required to reduce barriers to licensing and equity limits, for instance, but these two trends have spurred the growth in exports ahead of the trade agreements.[54]

Servcorp, one of Australia's largest exporters of services to Japan, provides serviced offices without an FTA covering services. For 20 years, Servcorp has invested in Japan, purchasing offices and leasing the space. This does not diminish the need for Australia to upgrade our institutional capacity as many modern services cannot be provided without a sovereign licence or authorisation.

North Asian trade agreements: unbundling the export of services

Australia has 10 bilateral free trade agreements, three agreed in 2014 with the North Asian powerhouses of China, Japan and South Korea. The North Asian FTAs appear to be the first where services have been given serious treatment alongside mining and farming.

The China Australia Free Trade Agreement (ChAFTA) was the first broad-based trade agreement China has struck with a major services

---

[54] Mark Thirlwell, interview, 29 June 2016.

economy. It contains a number of rare services commitments. It has many critics from trade academics to CFMEU and ETU officials but much of the critique is misguided. ChAFTA includes market access commitments for legal, education, telecommunications, financial, health and aged care, architecture, engineering, transport and mining services. More recent agreements China has struck with large services economies, such as South Korea in 2015, have limited or non-existent services market access commitments. Schott and Jung of the East Asia Forum expressed 'disappointment' with the bilateral agreement between Seoul and Beijing, saying: 'Market access negotiations on investment and services have also been deferred until at least 2018.'[55] ANU's Shiro Armstrong has been disappointed that both the Chinese bilateral deals with Australia and Korea are underwhelming. Armstrong wrote: 'Delaying negotiations on investment and services agreements between China and South Korea is exactly what Australia and China also did in their bilateral agreement, ChAFTA.'[56]

This does not stand up to scrutiny: the China-Australia agreement includes a wide range of services and in each Australia has been given an opportunity to access the world's second biggest economy with a growing middle class, while the Korean-China deal is limited to financial services and telecommunications. Alan Oxley notes: 'The China FTA goes further on services than other FTAs China has signed to date. In some areas, China has not placed restrictions on ownership – an indication China wishes to improve the contribution from services to the GDP.'[57]

---

[55] Jeffrey J. Schott and Euijin Jung, PIIE, 'South Korea–China FTA falls short on reform', *East Asia Forum*, 29 May, 2016.
[56] Shiro Armstrong, East Asia Forum Newsletter, 30 May 2016.
[57] Alan Oxley, interview, 7 July 2016.

The Japan Australia Economic Partnership Agreement (JAEPA) covers legal, financial, education, telecommunications and selected professional services.

The Korea Australia Free Trade Agreement (KAFTA) includes commitments for accountancy, environmental, engineering, legal, financial, education, telecommunications and selected professional services.

All these commitments require follow-through to deliver benefits and they can be forgotten or misunderstood. The CFMEU, for example, argued one of the reasons ChAFTA should be rejected is China has too many tariffs remaining in place and therefore Australia has been played for a fool. Comparing tariffs may have been a valid consideration in the Menzies era when trade agreements were struck and GATT was in full swing but it is an invalid comparison today given tariffs are not barriers to the export of services.

Australia has a number of comparative advantages in services but as Craig Dunn, a former CEO of AMP, chairman of FinTech hub Stone & Chalk and a director of Westpac and Telstra, says:

> Before you export anything, you need an internationally recognised or competitive product or service. Having a local market is a prerequisite to global success. You have to be competitive at home before you can do anything offshore. And perhaps we should allow others into our services sector on a unilateral basis to improve our competitiveness at home.[58]

Moufarrige says developing a competitive domestic market is a prerequisite for global success: 'The tax and regulatory systems should drive industry sectors that are nimble and competitive.'[59]

---

[58] Craig Dunn, interview with the author, July 2016.
[59] Moufarrige, *op. cit.*

Different sub-sectors highlight the diverse opportunities and challenges facing Australia as a fledgling services exporter.

Financial services

Australia's funds management industry is efficient and comparatively inexpensive. Financial services is Australia's largest industry, almost 10 per cent of GDP, but just 1 per cent of exports. The sector has untapped comparative advantages: Australia has the fourth largest pool of managed funds in the world yet we source more than 95 per cent of these funds from domestic investors (primarily superannuation funds).

Source of funds under management in Singapore

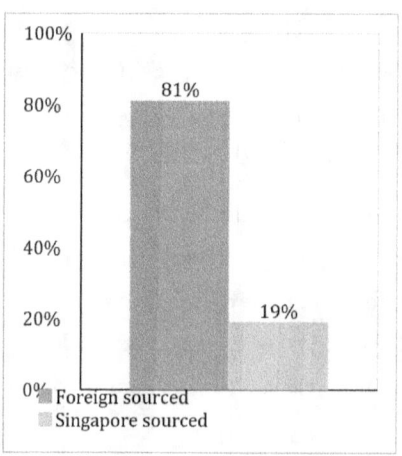

Source: Monetary Authority of Singapore, Singapore Asset Management Survey (2014)

Source of funds under management in Australia

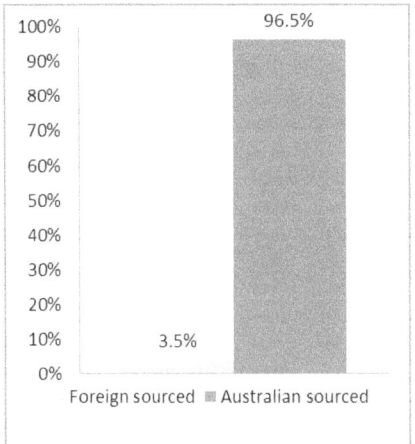

Source: Australian Bureau of Statistics 'Managed funds' (5655.0, September 2015)

Yet despite a landmark report by former Macquarie Bank deputy chairman Mark Johnson in 2009, *Building on our strengths: Australia as a financial centre*, we have not captured the opportunities. The sector is hampered by implementation challenges and needs domestic regulatory dynamism and competitiveness. Public policy in large regional financial centres is designed to attract foreign investment into managed funds. If we could increase foreign funds under management to the levels achieved by Singapore levels it would boost GDP by $4.2 billion, increase tax revenue by $1.2 billion and create 10,000 jobs.[60]

The 2009 Johnson Review (updated in June 2016) recommended policy reforms to increase competitiveness. The key barriers to increasing foreign funds under management are Australia's withholding tax regime and our high level of regulation which limits permissible investment structures. Fixing the withholding tax regime for offshore investors, which raises virtually no revenue and is incredibly complex to

---

[60] Deloitte Access Economics 'Impact of increasing exports of funds management', 2014

navigate, is a top priority.[61] The rate of withholding tax depends on:

- the country an investor resides in;
- whether a double tax agreement with Australia exists;
- the type of double tax agreement; and
- the type of assets in the investment.

While our competitors have withholding tax regimes which have been standardised or abolished in the case of Singapore, our boondoggle repels investors.

Australian fund managers also need a wider range of legal investment structures. The Corporations Act 2001 limits them to a 'unit-trust' legal structure which many foreign investors reject. Non-common law nations are not familiar with trust law so a broader range of investment structures, as announced in the 2016-17 budget, is essential.

A key Johnson report recommendation was that to export fund management services you need regulatory architecture. It recommended the creation of an 'Asian Region Funds Passport' (ARFP), allowing fund managers in the Asian region to trade across borders – a Sydney-based fund manager could sell a managed fund product, say, international shares or bonds to a resident in Tokyo or Seoul. The ARFP represents intangible trade architecture for managed funds in the same way the North Asian FTAs create broader services opportunities. ChAFTA provided preferential access to China's markets available to a very limited number of countries.

China has two schemes for trade and investment. Both have quotas as China is carefully managing the internationalisation of its currency and economy. Australia has access to both. The Qualified Domestic Institutional Investor (QDII) allows Chinese investors to trade

---

[61]   Mark Johnson AO, 'Australia as a Financial Centre', 2016.

offshore with foreign fund managers from Australia, among others. ChAFTA allows Australian fund managers market access to China to sell to QDII investors. There are 132 approved QDII (institutional investors) firms in China, which Australian fund managers can access. Second, the Renminbi Qualified Foreign Institutional Investor (RQFII) and predecessor, Qualified Foreign Institutional Investor (QFII) scheme, allow foreign investment into China. When the agreement was struck in November 2014 only 12 countries had RQFII quotas, including Australia. By June 2016, the number had risen to more than 20, including the US, the world's largest asset management market. RQFII guarantees access for Australian fund managers to Chinese share and bond markets.

The free trade agreement allows Australian securities firms to hold up to 49 per cent foreign equity (above its WTO commitment of 33 per cent) in joint ventures. These Australian institutions will gain access to underwriting for 'A', 'B' and 'H' shares beating the US and Japan. These quota-based systems and ownership ceilings are closer to a tariff on beef than they are to most services trade commitments as they are clear, hard coded and begin immediately. Chinese commitments for fund managers are lucrative and uncomplicated compared to Japanese and Korean commitments on access to their large asset management markets. The challenge is turning KAFTA and JAEPA commitments into market access. The language is problematic; for example, the agreements refer to 'portfolio management services' which do not exist in Australian law. The slow implementation of the Johnson Report's recommendations is regrettable. Craig Dunn, former CEO of major fund manager AMP says, 'funds management is a good example of a missed opportunity because Australia uses legal concepts which don't translate and tax arrangements which aren't competitive'.[62]

---

[62]   Dunn, *op.cit.*

Information and communications technology

Information and communications technology (ICT) employs more than 500,000 Australians and plays a critical role in the development of innovative potentially tradeable services. ICT accounts for up to 16 per cent of GDP adjusting ABS data.[63] It includes:

> telecommunications, internet-based data processing, storage and transmission, data processing and web hosting services, and computer system design and related services such as software development and installation. These businesses enable other businesses by providing a communications platform that allows business-to-business and business-to-customer interaction as well as advanced data processing and hosting services.[64]

ICT achieved the highest growth in the past decade among services enablers:

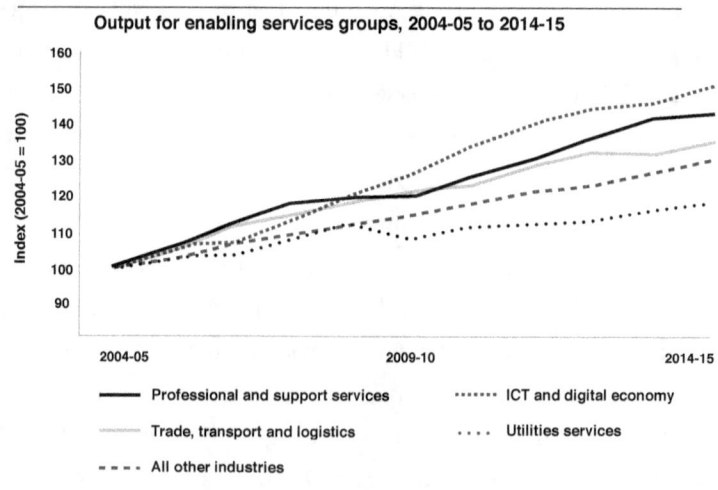

Output for enabling services groups, 2004-05 to 2014-15

Source: Industry Department

It is a diverse grouping with numerous subsectors.

---

[63] Australian Computer Society.

[64] Australian Department of Industry - Industry Report 2015, p. 68.

FinTech

Financial technology (FinTech) is transforming our financial system by reducing information asymmetry, mitigating risk and promoting the efficient allocation of scarce resources. This drives improvements in traditional financial services and promotes innovative new products and services, which offer benefits to consumers and other sectors of the economy.[65]

FinTech illustrates how domestic regulation determines competitiveness, fitness to trade and highlights the unsustainability of paper documents as trade agreements. The 2014 Financial System Inquiry recommended technology neutral language in domestic regulation and lamented the absence of technology neutral language in the Corporations Act (2001) which makes paper compulsory in transactions in a digital age. In response, in October 2015, the Government agreed to amend priority areas of legislation and regulation to make them technology neutral.[66]

A major challenge for FinTech is that regulation makes it hard to test ideas even when capital is available; innovators need to get ideas to market quickly not wait for the law to change. The UK created a 'regulatory sandbox' to test new ideas in a protected environment in late 2014 creating a 'safe space' for business to test innovative products, services, business models and delivery mechanisms in a live environment without immediately incurring the normal regulatory consequences of engaging in the activity in question.[67]

The 'regulatory sandbox' concept is being copied by Australia and Singapore. In mid-2016, the Australian Securities and Investment

---

[65]   Australian Government, 'Backing Australian Fintech', http://fintech.treasury.gov.au
[66]   Australian Government, 'Government Response to the Financial System Inquiry: Improving Australia's Financial System'.
[67]   Financial Conduct Authority, Regulatory sandbox, 11 May, 2015.

Commission was consulting on the design and said the changes would lower the barriers to entry faced by FinTech start-ups, reducing cost and promoting efficiency while maintaining the fundamental principles of the regulatory and licensing framework. It said the proposed licensing exemption compared favourably with other countries and would allow FinTechs to test some products without a detailed assessment by a regulator.[68]

Reference to competitiveness is highly unusual for an Australian regulator such as ASIC. The consultation process can yield a narrow sandbox. Natural regulatory conservatism must be set aside to allow FinTech to flourish. The question is where the line falls. We must embrace managed risk.

The Singaporeans announced their sandbox in June 2016 demonstrating their determination to be globally competitive and manage risk saying: 'There may be circumstances where it is less clear whether a particular FinTech solution complies with regulatory requirements or poses unacceptable risks.' But they are prepared to accept the uncertainty rather than 'stifle promising innovations' which 'may result in missed opportunities'.

Stone & Chalk, an industry-led FinTech hub, established in 2015 to help Australian start-ups become commercially viable, helped convince the Turnbull government that regulation can destroy opportunities, informing its innovation policy and the creation of the regulatory sandbox and the FinTech Advisory Council, chaired by the Treasurer. Australia is well-positioned to capture the next wave of growth. Stone & Chalk chairman Craig Dunn says:

> If you look at FinTech, we're using our strong financial services

---

[68]   Media release, 'Why the Fintech Regulatory Sandbox is a Game Changer', 8 June 2016.

brand to create the next generation of export opportunities. Australia is in a strong position in FinTech because the gap between consumer expectation and services provided is very small. The gap is not that great compared to other markets. We do very well in adopting new technology.[69]

There are very few times when Australia has been ahead of Singapore on a competitiveness measure but we are three months ahead on the sandbox which allows ideas to get to market as fast, or faster than Singapore and the UK. Marcus Moufarrige says, 'Singapore has always had a vision for business and exports. It's been a critical part of their success.' Singapore should be our benchmark.

With one of only three sandboxes (Australia, the UK, Singapore), Australia's approach to FinTech is the reverse of its slow efforts to improve competitiveness in financial services (funds management). The sandbox will prove its worth if FinTechs can create and export new services ahead of Singapore and the UK.

Tyro Payments, Australia's fastest growing EFTPOS provider told the Productivity Commission review of data availability and usage that investment in FinTech has started. In 2015, global investment in FinTech hit $US20 billion, a sevenfold increase in three years.[70] As well as attracting investment into new FinTech concepts, the other test is whether we can hold the maturing businesses in Australia. Australia has already lost CoinJar, which has moved to London and RISQ has moved to multiple locations in Asia.

---

[69] Dunn, *op.cit.*
[70] Jerome Doraisamy, 'Australia's fintech standing under threat', 5 July 2016, *Financial Observer*.

AgTech

Agricultural services use technological innovation to build on a traditional trading strength. AgTech start-up Full Profile uses blockchain distributed ledger technology to overhaul payment, providence and competition arrangements in grain production. Blockchain addresses a multitude of market, regulatory and farm gate issues grain producers' face. *Harvard Business Review* writes:

> Blockchain is a vast, global distributed ledger or database running on millions of devices and open to anyone, where not just information but anything of value – money, titles, deeds, music, art, scientific discoveries, intellectual property, and even votes – can be moved and stored securely and privately. On the Blockchain, trust is established, not by powerful intermediaries like banks, governments and technology companies, but through mass collaboration and clever code. Blockchain ensure integrity and trust between strangers. They make it difficult to cheat.[71]

Full Profile managing director Bob McKay believes Blockchain will 'allow farmers to get paid immediately, remove credit risk, a bigger market emerges and removes the need to fund collective bureaucracies to sell wheat'.

By establishing trust immediately, it obviates the need for ancient payment terms for farmers which have been based around an uncertain model of 21 or 30 days. In terms of providence, it traces and includes environmental standards and labels.

As Bob McKay said:

> (Our idea) creates a bigger market at the farm gate by linking

---

[71]   Don Tapscott and Alex Tapscott, 'The Impact of the Blockchain Goes Beyond Financial Services', 10, May, 2016, *Harvard Business Review*.

trusted buyers to sellers by using technology to eliminate the market problems of the past. The distributed ledger technology would remove the middle layer of industry collectives and bureaucracy.[72]

What is the role of government? A clear policy for competitiveness, testing in a safe environment and a recognition that start-ups cannot compete easily with established businesses.

Emma Weston says:

> the problem is the business hasn't yet been tested. It is extremely hard to test ideas in Australia. If we can't become a test bed for new ideas, we risk losing the developed ideas in agricultural technology to North America, where the technical capacity is matched with experience in agriculture and crucially, the ability to test things.[73]

If these ideas are tested and pioneered in Canada rather than Australia they risk becoming Canadian exports. A sandbox to test Australian innovation would give AgTech the opportunities enjoyed by FinTech. To win we need to innovate to create commercial advantages and test those innovations but the ability of the AgTech sector to advocate for this change is virtually non-existent. As Weston says: 'As a start-up, you cannot write a 100-page submission to a government consultation.'[74]

Queensland-based robotics company Swarmfarm established by grain, wheat and cattle farmer Andrew Bates uses small, lightweight, low-cost autonomous machines to perform a multitude of agricultural tasks:

> What we are looking at is swarms of small, lightweight machines that work together in a cooperative team. So instead of one large tractor, you might have six small ones about the size of a ride-on lawn mower.

---

[72]   Bob McKay, interview, July 2016.
[73]   Emma Weston, interview, July 2016.
[74]   *ibid.*

Everyone is getting bigger and bigger machines ... the damage they are doing to the soil is enormous ... we are trying to pull out a splinter with a set of fencing plier; we should be using tweezers.[75]

Bates has successfully developed farming robots through research, development and commercialisation. He identifies two problems:

Firstly, universities are provided with significant grants but the research tends to pile up rather than develop – there is a tendency to accumulate intellectual property. Second, the universities and many of the publicly funded development corporations do not want to deal with start-ups. They want John Deere. They don't want risk. The culture of the universities is to stick with the big end of town which means many ideas leave Australia to be developed despite our strength in robotics.[76]

Despite significant public investment in AgTech and strong competition from North America, there has been insufficient support for the commercialisation of innovative research. The Rural Research and Development for Profit scheme, announced in 2014, seeks to address that by providing almost $200 million to enhance the 'innovation of products, processes and practices across the food and fibre supply chains through technologies such as robotics, digitisation, big data, genetics and precision agriculture'.[77] Setting markers for the scheme's success should include tracking the balance of funds which support start-ups as opposed to established organisations and how much research is commercialised. Matthew Pryor argues we face stiff competition from Israel and New Zealand and we have recently seen examples such as AgDNA, a satellite based auto-steering of farm machinery firm, move to the U.S. Pryor argues we must be methodical

---

75   Amy McCosker, 'Farm robots soon to be a reality', 17 July 2013, ABC Rural.
76   Andrews Bates, Interview with the Author, 8 July 2016.
77   Australian Government Department of Agriculture and Water Resources, 'Rural Research and Development for Profit'.

in our approach to AgTech. In his words:

> It is worth remembering that Australia didn't become a world
> leader in iron ore in a few short years. Securing a long term and
> profitable place in the emerging market for AgTech will require
> both the long view and targeted policy.[78]

There are other opportunities to support innovation in Australia. We have a strong ICT sector which can support innovation in medical technology. Across the board, we need a framework where Australia can pioneer, commercialise and export concepts. This will be a key test of success of the the 2015 Commonwealth Innovation Statement.

Professional services

Professional services including engineering, legal, accounting and architecture are treated haphazardly in the North Asian FTAs. This approach doesn't do justice to our strengths in these sectors: an internationally respected legal framework, world-class universities and highly competitive domestic markets. We need to unbundle the opportunities and better understand the barriers to export for each service.

Legal services

There are almost 70,000 practicing solicitors in Australia.[79] Australia is a common law country which is an advantage with former British Empire countries such as Hong Kong, India and Singapore, as it

---

[78] Matthew Pryor, 'Can Australia be a global leader in AgTech?', National Farmers' Federation, 7 August 2016.
[79] 2014 Law Society National Profile, Final Report, April 2015, Prepared by Urbis for The Law Society of New South Wales.

increases compatibility and transferability of skills. However, common law can present an insurmountable challenge in other jurisdictions which operate under the 'code' system – widely found in North Asia. There are significant shortfalls in the legal profession in compatible nations such as India where there are only 600,000 lawyers, six lawyers per 10,000 people, and vastly less than a developed nation.[80] Unusually in the global context, Australian lawyers are not registered with the national government because Australia is a federation and lawyers are effectively regulated by the states and territories.

KAFTA opens the door for Australian lawyers in three steps: representative offices were permitted from 2014; cooperative agreements between Korean and Australian law firms are permitted from the end of 2016; and new joint ventures can begin in 2019. A Law Council fact sheet says KAFTA removed the shackles where previously only around 50 Australian lawyers were permitted to 'advise'.

The Korean FTA provides the piece of the puzzle that only government-to-government negotiations can deliver. It is the 'third stage' commitment from 2019 permitting Australians to establish law firms in Korea which significantly removes protection:

> The enhancement in legal service opportunities complements the Law Council's long-standing relationship with the Korean Bar Association. In 1998 the Law Council and the Korean Bar Association signed a Memorandum of Understanding recognising the growing importance of trade and other ties between the two countries and the vital role played by the legal profession in facilitating these relationships.[81]

---

[80]   Asher Judah, *The Australian Century*, (Connor Court, 2014) p. 23.
[81]   Law Council of Australia, Media Release, 'Law Council Welcomes Legal Service Opportunities through KAFTA,' 17 February 2014.

The amended Korean Foreign Legal Consultants Act allows Australian law firms to set up partnerships and is identical to the agreement the EU has with Korea except that the EU's 'phase three' access began on 1 July 2016. The Law Council of Australia (LCA) is pushing to accelerate the timetable to pare back the EU's first-mover advantage.

The Japanese FTA contains less detailed commitments stating only that Australian companies can operate 'Legal Professional Corporations' and that the LCA and Japanese Bar Association will be tasked with determining mutual recognition. A Law Council report says establishing a business in Japan is an 'administratively intensive process' and registration as a foreign lawyer is extremely complicated.[82] It explains:

> As a foreign lawyer, you can assist local lawyers in doing work but you can't actually give legal advice, so to the extent that you want to actually do anything substantial for local clients or involving Japanese law, you really need some local Japanese lawyers … you have to pass quite a difficult exam if you want to actually get that qualification and not a lot of people do it.[83]

The commitments for the LCA and Japanese Bar Association to pursue mutual recognition does not allow the establishment of legal practices as does the Korean agreement but the LCA and the Bar Association have started negotiations on a mutual recognition framework.

ChAFTA contains specific commitments, allowing Australian lawyers access to the Shanghai Free Trade Zone (SFTZ). The Law

---

[82]　Law Council of Australia: Submission to Productivity Commission inquiry into barriers to services exports, 2015, p. 37.
[83]　*Ibid.*, p. 19.

Council of Australia said:

> The positive elements of the (S)FTZ related commitment include:
> the right to work in association with Chinese lawyers to provide
> legal services from the one source covering both Chinese and
> foreign law; the right to provide those services to clients within
> and outside the (S)FTZ; and the capacity to maintain a level of
> independence between the Australian and local firms, particularly
> in the use of firm names and the flow of liabilities.[84]

Australia has a significant first-mover advantage as the EU and US
have limited access to Chinese markets but to provide genuine market
access Australia must liberalise a raft of complicated requirements
foreign lawyers face.

On legal services alone, we have three different types of
commitments in the North Asian FTAs. The follow-through on each
FTA will be different, with only the Korean agreement having dates
to act as a clear road map.

Engineering

There are more than 100,000 engineers in Australia registered using
a state-based legal framework with no mandatory registration except
in Queensland. By contrast, Japan and Korea require engineers to
register with government. Engineers Australia (EA) has long been
aware of this difference and supports mandatory registration of
engineers to align with our trading partners. Since 2015, engineers
can register with Engineers Australia.

Engineering is a mixed bag in the North Asian agreements. JAEPA

---

[84]   Martyn Hagan, Letter to the Committee Secretary Joint Standing Committee on
Treaties, 24 July 2015.

guarantees 'existing market access' for engineers, ChAFTA provides a specific commitment that engineers can access the SFTZ and KAFTA provides an avenue for mutual recognition.

EA moved at lightening pace. In 2015 it made good on the commitment in KAFTA to allow Australian engineers to access the Korean market by signing a mutual recognition agreement with the Korean and Australian governments. Engineers Australia CEO said: 'This Mutual Recognition Agreement means that the qualifications and expertise of Australian engineers will be formally recognised should they practice in South Korea.'

Mutual recognition allows chartered engineers listed in EA's national register to provide services in Korea without supervision or being in partnership and Australian chartered engineers are recognised as local Korean engineers. This was achieved just six months after the FTA was signed thanks to a strong, forward-looking professional body working with its membership and engaging with home and host government.

Consult Australia CEO Megan Motto said:

> Mutual recognition is particularly important for professional services … in some countries as there is a requirement for registration or certification to run a company or sign off on drawings. We need international standards programs. At home, although we have a national building code, we have special regulations in each state and territory which can diminish international comparability and add unnecessary complexity. Services are sold on relationships not at a trade booth. Reputation and trust are not transactional – it is unsuited to traditional trade facilitation.[85]

---

[85]   Megan Motto, Interview with Author, 13 July 2016.

The benefits are tangible. As Andrew Robb commented:

> Engineering, construction and architecture have been significant beneficiaries of the Closer Economic Relations program of mutual recognition with New Zealand. Ninety per cent of Christchurch reconstruction services were won by Australian companies because mutual recognition had driven harmonised building codes. It made it seamless. It's a great example of effective mutual recognition.[86]

Architecture

Australia's 12,000 architects register with statutory-backed, state registration boards. To improve transferability of skills, state registration boards established the Architects Accreditation Council of Australia, which maintains national standards and qualifications. The AACA works with the Australian Institute of Architects on the accreditation of domestic architecture programs. Both organisations are involved in international trade and policy.

The AACA assesses overseas architectural qualifications registration in Australia and/or migration eligibility through a two-stage Overseas Qualifications Assessment. It is also the lead organisation for the negotiation of international mutual recognition arrangements.[87]

KAFTA does not contain any commitments on architecture. ChAFTA allows for the establishment of Australian-owned businesses and provides for mutual recognition. JAEPA opens the door for mutual recognition of qualifications.

---

[86]   Andrew Robb, Interview with Author, 28 June 2016.
[87]   The Architects Accreditation Council of Australia, 'About Us', http://www.aaca.org.au/about-us/

Architecture is unusual because a lot of work has already been done within APEC on mutual recognition of registration and to standardise education. Under the APEC agreement, a bilateral or multilateral agreement (such as the trilateral agreement between Australia, New Zealand and Singapore) will create genuine market access.

The 2008 'Canberra Accord' between Australia, Canada, China, Korea, Japan, Mexico and the US also lays the groundwork for an internationally recognised base of architectural education but it does not allow market access or ownership.

Australia and Japan have a decade-old mutual recognition arrangement for the registration of architects under the APEC framework but it is cumbersome and should be updated in the wake of the FTA.

The China commitment has little value until a system of architectural registration is established in China. Without that, there is no way to agree on equivalency. The Australian Institute of Architects says:

> ChAFTA cannot provide for mutual recognition of qualifications or rights to practice, as each province within China has different registration requirements and there is no way to determine the standard of qualifications – this would have to be done on a university by university basis as there is no overall accreditation system in place.[88]

AACA CEO Kate Doyle says: 'Unless you have an industry basis for mutual recognition, the government-to-government discussions are basically useless.'

---

[88]   Institute of Architects, email to the Author, 20 July 2016.

Accounting

JAEPA and ChAFTA contain nothing specific for accountants. KAFTA allows members of CPA Australia or the Institute of Chartered Accountants to practise accountancy via a local entity and invest and work in Korea by 2019. There is also a commitment to secure mutual recognition via the professional bodies.

A working group on professional services from KAFTA met in mid-2016 for government-to-government discussions which don't include industry stakeholders. So little industry engagement almost two years after KAFTA is a wasted opportunity. It is unlikely there is little interest in Korea. Unfortunately, the agreement provides a glacial three-year timetable to progress the commitment:

> The parties hereby establish a Working Group on Professional Services, comprising representatives of each party, to facilitate the activities (such as accounting) ... The Working Group shall meet within three years after the date of entry into force of this Agreement unless the parties otherwise agree.[89]

Accountancy is underpinned by global standards in education, competency and often, regulation through international accounting standards. These standards have no impact on investment, ownership and the ability of foreign entities to conduct business in a host jurisdiction. Trade agreements need to specifically address these matters.

International Federation of Accountants president Rachel Grimes says effective accountancy agreements are possible and the North American FTA (NAFTA) provides the benchmark for professional services and accountancy as it unbundles each service and provides investment and market access.

---

[89]   KAFTA Annex 7A

This overview of four professional services exports highlights how little use there is for an umbrella term. We need to unpack each service export opportunity as we do for each commodity export. Lawyers and engineers have done the most work, probably because these professions have the most to gain from the trade deals. Both sectors have strong industry bodies which have swiftly progressed commitments. In architecture, the industry can only achieve mutual recognition if the profession in the host nation is organised and able to engage with another nation's professional body. Accountants simply haven't focused on implementing trade commitments.

Improving services implementation: creating a new framework

Australia can beat advanced services-based economies to the Asian giants through bilateral trade agreements. The North Asian trade deals provide the first opportunity to turn broad services commitments into genuine market access. To do this we need to change domestic policy and follow through with our trading partners. The challenges are immense: addressing them requires a practical framework to complement market proximity and dynamic trade agreements.

Frame the challenges

First we need a framework for services trade implementation that:

- removes uniquely Australian regulatory terminology, aligning trade language with regulated terms and avoiding language which can be 'disrupted';

- ends open-ended services commitments by incorporating a time table for each commitment;

- builds mutual recognition capacity for professional/industry self-regulation and regulatory recognition purposes;
- includes services sector representatives in negotiations; and
- increases reporting requirements and accountability to ensure progress can be monitored.

Manage the language

Language is everything in free trade agreements. Three changes are required.

First, reduce Australian-specific naming conventions and regulated terminology to boost compatibility and export prospects. Korean and Japanese FTAs refer to 'portfolio management services' which is not used in any jurisdiction. It is legacy trade language which was used before we recognised financial services had become a comparative advantage. We should use the globally accepted term – 'mutual funds'. The problem is that even though 'mutual funds' is the accepted global term for managed funds, we use the term 'managed investment scheme'. We should change our 'managed investment scheme' terminology, even though we have the fourth largest market because it does not serve our interests in a globalised world. The Financial System Inquiry of 2014 reported: 'Policy makers should avoid adopting unique Australian regulatory approaches that are inconsistent with international practice.'[90] If we must stick to the unsatisfactory use of trade language and we cannot change long-standing domestic regulatory definitions, each FTA should have a translation schedule. This would allow businesses to immediately see what has been agreed.

---

[90]   Financial System Inquiry 2014, Australian Government, p.36.

Second, trade language should be aligned with regulatory language. Using trade boffin language complicates 'follow-through' work and can be confusing to market participants accustomed to the language associated with their licensing and regulatory framework. Cox Architects said to the Productivity Commission:

> Government goes to great trouble, often over many years, to establish free trade agreements with other countries. But little work is done to explain the possibilities that may flow from these agreements. This is particularly an issue for professional services where the trade 'language' is not understood and the opportunities not clear.[91]

Similarly, the Australian Information Industry Association said:

> trade agreements are not fully utilised and typically not widely understood by the business sector. Key barriers to their use include the complexity of agreement terms; the limited nature of some agreements – with a focus primarily on tariff reduction rather than issues such as e-commerce, intellectual property, trade in services etc.[92]

Hard-won commitments can be lost because of language. If we want to export managed funds, we should use the language used in our laws. A pan-Asian study by the Economist Intelligence Unit said 45 per cent of companies sampled attributed the low utilisation rates of FTAs in our region to 'the complexity of the agreements themselves, which comprise hundreds of pages of dense legal text, annexes and tariff schedules.'[93]

---

[91] Cox Architects, Submission to Productivity Commission barriers to exports of services
[92] Barriers to Services Exports: Productivity Commission Issues Paper AIIA response, p. 9.
[93] The Economist Intelligence Unit 'FTAs: Fantastic, Fine or Futile', 2016, p. 8.

Three, we must avoid language which can be easily 'disrupted' by technological change. Trade agreements should be principles-based so that they can deal with new products and services; if they are too narrowly focused on specific products and services they can quickly become outdated.

Paper-based trade agreements in the digital age are ripe for disruption. A dynamic review process and a principles-based approach to accommodate technological change is essential. As Emma Weston says: 'The pace of change is breathtaking and tomorrow needs to be next week.' A recent report by A.T. Kearney predicts a Silicon Valley Earthquake which will disrupt every Australian industry[94] through the application of research iPCn genomics, artificial intelligence, advanced robotics and autonomous vehicles.

Impose timetables

Many services commitments do not have timetables which leads to drift and minimises accountability. An implementation timetable puts pressure on regulators, industry participants and governments to deliver.

The open-ended architecture commitment in the Japan FTA is a good example of an arrangement we would never make for a tariff for a hard commodity but no-one can argue with the firm commitment provided in KAFTA for Australian lawyers; three clear dates for the removal of protections. The Law Council says this has already piqued the interest of Australians eyeing the Korean market. This should be a timetable template for every new services commitment. In contrast, the rubbery KAFTA commitment for accountants to establish a

---

[94]   A.T. Kearney, 'Australia: Taking Bigger Steps', 2016.

working group within three years should not be repeated. We must do better than giving ourselves three years to agree to have a meeting.

Achieving mutual recognition

Achieving effective mutual recognition is the services economy equivalent of cutting or abolishing a tariff in the resources sector. The capacity for mutual recognition has been included in each North Asian FTA.   Numerous PC studies have found that barriers to services are often not dealt with in FTAs, relying instead on mutual recognition:[95]

> It is difficult to directly address all behind-the-border barriers to services trade through trade agreements given the range of rules and regulations that govern service provision. Trade agreements can, however, provide a framework to progress further liberalisation and to establish supplementary measures such as mutual recognition agreements (MRAs) or standards harmonization…[96]

Mutual recognition in professional services (such as legal, financial and architectural firms) can be more flexible and less subject to sovereign risk because the requirements for registration and professional practice are set by professional associations rather than governments. There are two types of mutual recognition - regulatory mutual recognition and industry mutual recognition.

---

[95]   See for instance 2010 and 2014 reviews by Productivity Commission (p. 74, 2013-14 T and A) and Productivity Commission 2015 review into mutual recognition
[96]   Productivity Commission inquiry into services exports, p.26.

Regulatory mutual recognition

Regulatory mutual recognition occurs when a regulator recognises a foreign legal regime. It delivers market access and increases capacity in markets with lower standards. The PC writes:

> By reducing regulatory compliance costs for service providers, mutual recognition agreements (MRAs) can help facilitate market access and promote competition between local and foreign providers. Consumers can benefit from greater choice of service providers and from lower prices. Another potential benefit arises from the examination of the differences in regulation between countries that occurs during the process of establishing an MRA and determining equivalence of licensing arrangements.[97]

Effective mutual recognition enlarges markets and drives higher standards. It should have higher visibility in the coverage in trade deals as raising capacity has geopolitical value. The problem is often the political interest in achieving market access through mutual recognition can fall away once the politicians have attended the signing ceremony and tariffs on tradeable goods have been removed. Resources must be channelled into implementation before moving to the next round of FTAs, yet on the back of the deals already signed by Australia in the past three years, we are already progressing another handful.

The Hong Kong/Australia agreement to allow mutual recognition of managed fund operators has failed to deliver on its promise. It was announced by the Securities and Financial Commission of Hong Kong and the Australian Securities and Investments Commission in 2008 with great fanfare. ASIC said:

---

[97] Productivity Commission inquiry into mutual recognition, ibid., p. 261.

Not only does it present exciting marketing opportunities for our respective funds management industry seeking investment flows from the counterpart jurisdiction, it also gives more choices to the Australian and Hong Kong retail public.[98]

Minister Nick Sherry added:

Mutual recognition would benefit Australian retail investors because they would have access to a broader choice of financial products while Australian managed investment schemes would be relieved from a wide range of Hong Kong regulatory requirements on the basis of their compliance with Australian requirements.[99]

Even the Investment and Financial Services Association was supportive. But despite the resources spent on securing the agreement not one financial services business has used the framework in the eight years since then.

This is not due to a lack of interest, it is because the agreement is complicated and needs providers to meet a range of requirements in the host jurisdiction, undermining the claim of 'mutual recognition'. It is a good example of an agreement which has failed because the regulators developed a framework without sufficient industry input to make the scheme a success.

We must get better at mutual recognition – it will be one of the most important disciplines in trade policy this century. The Productivity Commission (PC) has been studying mutual recognition in the context of the Closer Economic Relations (CER) between Australia and New Zealand for more than 30 years. It has recommended improvements to

---

[98] Australian Securities and Investments Commission, 'Australia and Hong Kong sign deal to allow cross-border marketing of retail funds', 7 July 2008.

[99] Nick Sherry, Minister for Superannuation and Corporate Law, Media Release, 'Mutual Recognition Agreement with Hong Kong', 7 July, 2008.

the CER mutual recognition framework which is designed to promote a common market between the two nations. When undertaking its review of barriers to services exports, it recommended sweeping changes to Australia's approach to mutual recognition:

> The Australian Government should put in place a framework to support the development of mutual recognition agreements as part of, or following, the inclusion of mutual recognition provisions in trade or other agreements. The framework should include clear actions and timeframes for an implementation working group (that is adequately resourced and involves relevant regulators and government bodies) to report on its progress to the committee responsible for overseeing implementation of the agreement. The framework should also include a process for consulting with industry stakeholders.

Mutual recognition has proven elusive in the context of FTAs because the committee process does not have a clear framework or a timetable or engage regulators and industry stakeholders but in recent years, DFAT has developed an innovative approach to support the committee process. Australia participated in services sector promotion forums in China and in 2014 and 2015, Korea and then Australia hosted forums designed to bring regulators, industry and government together in the financial, legal and construction services sectors. But although the meetings have been successful in bringing groups together there has not been enough focus on generating outcomes. Unless such forums result in genuine mutual recognition, there is little point in the process. To achieve regulatory mutual recognition, Australia should:

- adopt the PC recommendation on clear commitments, a timetable and industry involvement;

- establish a mutual recognition unit within government to facilitate this process;
- publish a roadmap for delivering commitments; and
- require regulators to periodically report on implementation progress and answer questions at Senate Estimates and Parliamentary oversight hearings.

In financial services, for example, recognition requires ASIC and the relevant foreign regulator issuing licensing relief and a regulatory guide for financial services licensees. An Australian licensee should be able to access a host market to sell products to resident investors under one licence. Ensuring a whole-of-government approach is critical. As Peter Varghese said:

> … policy making is a serious business. It should draw on evidence but it should also flow from a deep and broad understanding of our country and its history. Silos may work in agriculture but they are corrosive to good government.[100]

Industry mutual recognition

Industry mutual recognition occurs when a self-regulating industry body gains mutual recognition for its members under the auspices of a foreign government; it is the professional or industry association which accredits individual practitioners. Engineers Australia has established mutual recognition with Korea. Engineers Australia told the Productivity Commission:

> Australia's trade in engineering services would benefit considerably by increasing the importance of mutual recognition agreements

---

[100] Peter N Varghese AO, 'Parting Reflections Secretary's speech to IPAA Speech', 9 June 2016.

for professional services, and elevating the level at which they are dealt with, in all free trade agreements when they are revised as well as including them in new agreements. ... Arrangements relating to engineering vary considerably throughout the world: registration is mandatory in some countries and not in others; in some cases registration is the responsibility of State rather than national governments; alternatives to mandatory registration exist in some countries while in other cases there are no arrangements. Engineers Australia believes that the mobility of engineers and engineering services will be limited while this situation persists.

Industry-based recognition is harder for governments to drive but is no less important given Australia's strength in professional services. Trade agreements should specify the professional bodies required to implement the commitment using the template set in JAEPA in legal services where the relevant organisations are named.

Government should also collaborate with industries to ensure professions are globally compatible. Engineering shows what can be achieved when provincial Australian approaches are dropped in favour of a system that is globally understood.

In a sign that mutual recognition is slowly gaining prominence, the most recently updated trade agreement, the Australia-Singapore Comprehensive Strategic Partnership, included commitments for mutual recognition in engineering and accountancy. Andrew Robb sees mutual recognition as a growing 'core function' in the trade policy toolkit. Trade and Investment Minister Steve Ciobo says he will create a Professional Services Mutual Recognition Unit to provide direct assistance to professional associations and regulators in the negotiation of international recognition of Australian qualifications and licensing.[101] The Liberal Party's 2016 election document said:

> Without international authority to practise their profession, our accountants, architects, engineers, lawyers, physiotherapists, vets, teachers and others are often unable to provide their services to international clients, or to Australian clients with international operations. The Professional Services Mutual Recognition Unit will provide direct assistance to professional associations and regulators in negotiating the international recognition of Australian qualifications and licensing.[102]

Increasing industry involvement

On every front, more effective industry involvement is required. As the PC wrote:

> Several industry representatives, whilst welcoming DFAT's consultation efforts, called for a deeper role for business in the negotiation process. The Australian Services Roundtable stated that: Industry would welcome and seeks closer involvement during trade negotiations and alongside this involvement, industry would welcome being privy to information, texts, papers and progress reports during negotiations.[103]

The opacity of trade deals has long been criticised. Sovereign governments need to negotiate in secrecy given the sensitivities but government must bring industry closer to the negotiations while maintaining confidentiality. Rather than compromise sovereign negotiations, which would be counterproductive, we should adopt a system of detailed consultation with industry using confidentiality

---

[101] Hon Steve Ciobo, responses via email, 7 July 2016.
[102] Coalition trade policy statement on trade, July 2016.
[103] The Productivity Commission, Barriers to Services Exports, *op.cit.*

agreements. This allows industries to provide feedback on the language and offer a view on priority markets and barriers. Technical engagement with industry is required. Like John McEwen, Australia must bring the services industries into the tent.

Governance and reporting

Better governance of implementation and increased transparency is overdue. Committee processes need to be overhauled. Under KAFTA, for example, numerous committees and working groups meet periodically. Committees on trade in goods, energy and mineral resources cooperation, financial services and a working group on professional services reinforce the haphazard approach to services. The committees provide scant summaries of progress. For example, 18 months after KAFTA was signed, the first meeting of the financial services committee, held in April 2016, published a four-paragraph statement with no timetables for implementation or detail about how commitments would be implemented. Only one date was set – for the next committee meeting, 'in the first half of 2017'. This is patently inadequate; the committee process should be a standing engagement and regulators and professional/industry associations must be involved at all stages.

Greater transparency will put pressure on committees to deliver results. We should require periodic reporting to parliament on FTA services implementation, permit questions during Senate Estimates to regulators and require regulatory agencies to include implementation targets in their annual reports.

This framework should be implemented as the parliament's response to the Productivity Commission review of Services Exports and the Parliamentary Inquiry into Business Utilisation of FTAs. We need a services trade implementation agency, housed in DFAT, which formally involves regulators, industry bodies and market participants. The agency should focus on the major services commitments Australia secures in trade negotiations such as engineering, legal and financial services.

More bureaucracy is never the answer to a complex problem like services trade implementation but coordination is clearly lacking across government and a formal process need not be a bloated bureaucracy. The implementation agency should operate as a board with the heads of the regulators and industry bodies acting as directors and the chair accountable to parliament's committees.

Next opportunities: testing the new framework

Australia is in a fortunate position to test this framework. We are negotiating bilateral trade agreements with Indonesia and India, amongst others, and the largest plurilateral trade agreement in history, the Regional Comprehensive Economic Partnership (RCEP), is being negotiated by India, China, ASEAN, Australia and others. With an increasingly ambitious trade agenda, there are genuine avenues to test the framework on services trade.

We face significant hurdles in concluding the Trans Pacific Partnership in the current environment. Yet the TPP, or the even more ambitious Regional Comprehensive Economic Partnership, could be the big opportunity of the next decade. John Howard commented:

> I'm concerned there is a trend back to protectionism in the US and Europe. The EU has never been an advocate for open trade. The EU did a lot of damage to trade and to Australian exports.

No Australian should feel any warmth about the EU's trade policy. Trump is very protectionist ... That's why our FTAs are vital. Multilateral FTAs have run into the sand. The new bilateral agreements are very important and they have WTO principles. We should negotiate an FTA with the UK. It's all a question of mutual advantage. I'm a big believer in open trade, it's been of great advantage to Australia and lifted hundreds of millions of people out of poverty.[104]

Winning the argument on the merits of free trade may be as important as adopting the suggested changes to our approach. Trade Minister Steve Ciobo says the government remains committed to an ambitious agenda:

(There are) significant shifts in the global trade context which will provide additional head winds for future market access and domestic reform. Australia's open attitude to pursuing our national interest through trade is under threat. Despite Australia being the economic beneficiary of decades of trade engagement with the world, there are examples of those willing to challenge this orthodoxy. Examples include some of the US Presidential debates rhetoric as well as some of the discussion aired during the Brexit debate.

Analysis by the World Bank found countries that liberalised their trade regimes experienced average annual growth rates that were around 1.5 percentage points higher than before liberalisation. China's opening to the world over the past four decades has lifted hundreds of millions of people out of poverty.

In these fluid times, trade is more important than ever. We face the possible threat of trade hostilities between the US and China, the

---

[104] John Howard, interview with author, July 2016.

US withdrawal from the Trans Pacific Partnership and its potential replacement by the Regional Comprehensive Economic Partnership which includes China. We also need to rapidly negotiate a new trade relationship with post-Brexit Britain which will be both partner and competitor. The RCEP and the bilateral negotiations with India and Indonesia are the next cabs off the rank. We should place as much of the new services framework into the negotiations as possible.

In the face of uncertainty, our best insurance is to be as open, competitive and agile as possible. Being fit for service starts with the recognition that services exports are inherently harder to achieve than traditional physical exports. It also requires us to think of trade deals as the end of the beginning rather than the beginning of the end.

We will have to work harder than ever to exploit our advantages and service the growing Asian middle class. Our future prosperity depends on it.

Conclusion

NEXT STEPS

Recommendation 1: Australian business must develop stronger capacity to advocate the virtues of free trade and open markets

The arguments which were won in the 1980s against populism, protection and closed markets were won with the support of the NFF and MCA (AMIC). As it was then, business cannot expect better business conductions without advocacy. The business community must develop a vehicle for making the arguments for free trade, open markets and an agenda for competitiveness in tax and regulation. This role cannot be left to academics and think tanks. Business leaders who employ Australians must publicly support this agenda, otherwise we risk protection and populism taking hold.

Recommendation 2: Boost institutional capacity by gaining market proximity

Department of Foreign Affairs and Trade staff should be closer to dynamic industries. This should occur through embedding DFAT staff in businesses as these secondments would also improve market knowledge. At a minimum, Trade officials must develop experience and a perspective on disruptive technology.

After a reasonable period of time, DFAT should transparently publish the number of staff it has with experience in each industry sector.

Recommendation 3: Introduce dynamic digital agreements

Trade agreements should move from paper-based documents to a digital platform which contains general principles for market access. Given Australia has signed bilateral agreements with our leading trading partners, we should institute this process swiftly.

We should bring the FTA 'Committee' processes to light and convene standing meetings on implementation with permanent industry liaison for industries subject to rapid technological change.

Recommendation 4: ISDS should be strongly supported

Investor State Dispute Settlement is a mechanism which serves Australia's interests as an investor into the Asian region as a conscious act of sovereignty from the Australian government. ISDS should be retained, supported and improved in future trade agreements. The transparent tribunals operating under The Hague Convention and the World Bank used in the plain packaging cases against the Australian and Uruguayan governments should be maintained to resolve investment disputes. Further analysis from government bodies such as the Productivity Commission should consider outbound Australian foreign investment and the commercial ambitions of our nation in this century.

Recommendation 5: Adopt a new framework for services trade

A new framework for achieving genuine market access for services should be adopted. The framework contains the following elements:

- Removing uniquely Australian regulatory terminology, aligning trade language with regulated terms and avoiding language which can be 'disrupted';

- Ending the practice of open-ended services commitments by incorporating a timetable for each commitment;

- Building mutual recognition capacity for professional/industry self-regulation and regulatory recognition purposes;

- Including services sector representatives in the process of negotiation in true McEwen style; and

- Increasing reporting requirements and accountability to ensure implementation progress can be monitored

About the Author

Andrew Bragg is the director of policy and research at the Menzies Research Centre. He is also the head of the Enterprise Policy Unit which backs Australians taking risks to invest and employ people. An accountant by profession, Andrew spent the past three years as head of policy at the Financial Services Council, one of Australia's leading industry bodies. Andrew's passion for public policy stems from his belief a strong economy is the basis of a just and prosperous society.

He regularly contributes on economic issues in the *Australian Financial Review* and *The Australian* as well as on radio and television. Primarily Andrew researches and discusses budget management and taxation, federalism, competitiveness and trade, financial services as well as superannuation and demographic change. Andrew believes these economic policies should drive a competitive and sustainable nation for our children.

He is a married father who lives in Sydney, NSW, having grown up in country Victoria. Andrew enjoys fishing, football and reading. He isn't afraid to make the case for a stronger Australia on social media. You'll find him here: @ajamesbragg

Acknowledgements

My thanks go to Nick Cater for commissioning the project. The following people have been incredibly helpful in formulating the ideas, finding facts or reviewing drafts: Peter Morris, Jennifer Hewitt, David Crowe, Ben Heap, Spiro Premetis, James Brown, Alan Oxley, Mark Thirlwell, Luke Malpass and Adam Creighton. Thanks to those who helped edit the manuscript for publication: Rebecca Weisser, Karen Cross, Kay Gilchrist, Anthony Cappello and Michael Gilchrist. I'm extremely grateful to the interviewees which span Australia's political and business leadership. As readers will note, many fine Australians have given their time and have been generous with their insights. Finally I want to acknowledge the work of our foreign service. The officials from the Department of Foreign Affairs and Trade and Austrade remain amongst our best and brightest.

R. G. MENZIES ESSAYS OF IDEAS

Sir Robert Gordon Menzies kept a journal throughout his political life in which he would take notes of ideas, conversations and events.

The R. G. Menzies Essays of Ideas is published in the same spirit. It does not set out to be the last word on any given topic, merely a record of good ideas, articulately expressed, that may be enriched through further discussion. If you would like to contribute to the debate online, or submit a contribution for future volumes, email: correspondence@menziesrc.org

Menzies Research Centre
Chairman: Tom Harley
Executive Director: Nick Cater
Deputy Director: Kay Gilchrist
PO Box 6091
Kingston ACT 2604
email: correspondence@menziesrc.org
www.menziesrc.org

R. G. MENZIES ESSAYS OF IDEAS

VOLUME 1

QUIET ACHIEVERS:
THE NEW ZEALAND PATH TO REFORM

OLIVER HARTWICH

Do today's politicians have the courage to make hard choices? Or has the furious pace of modern politics put an end to the age of reform?

In *Quiet Achievers*, Oliver Hartwich looks at New Zealand's record on spending, tax and welfare.

He discovers that while Australia has been avoiding difficult decisions, the New Zealanders have been silently forging ahead.

Oliver Hartwich is Executive Director of The New Zealand Initiative.

Series Editor: Nick Cater

"A perceptive analysis of the Key playbook" – Ruth Richardson

"A message that resonates across the Tasman" – Henry Ergas

Available from: www.connorcourt.com

R. G. MENZIES ESSAYS OF IDEAS

VOLUME 2

ON FAIRNESS

EDITED BY NICK CATER

Egalitarianism is a cherished Australian value. But in its modern guise of 'fairness' it is corrupting political debate. *On Fairness* reveals how this fuzzy and contested concept leads governments astray. Liberty, rather than state control, provides the best path to a truly fair Australia.

Chapters include:
The Moral High Ground – Nick Cater
Envy Politics – Henry Ergas
Fairness, Family and Freedom – Kelly O'Dwyer
The Perils of Benevolence – Rebecca Weisser
Tax, Regulation and Poverty – Alexander Scaife
Conservative Social Justice – Iain Duncan Smith

Series Editor: Nick Cater

Available from: www.connorcourt.com

R. G. MENZIES ESSAYS OF IDEAS

Volume 3

Game Plan:

The Case for a New Australian Grand Strategy

Ross Babbage

The gravest duty of a government is not to balance the books. It is to protect its people.

But in an era of more challenging and complex threats, our greatest foe could be poor planning.

How can Australia avoid falling hostage to ad-hoc decisions, wasteful spending, bureaucratic inertia and fitful planning?

Game Plan argues for a new Grand Strategy – a blueprint to deter the next war, and, if forced to fight, to win.

Ross Babbage is a senior defence analyst and the head of Strategy International.

Series Editor: Nick Cater

Available from: www.connorcourt.com

R. G. MENZIES ESSAYS OF IDEAS

VOLUME 4

THE PROMISE OF DIGITAL GOVERNMENT: TRANSFORMING PUBLIC SERVICES, REGULATION, AND CITIZENSHIP

ANGUS TAYLOR

Digital disruption is transforming the marketplace and improving our lives in ways we never imagined.

Angus Taylor says it is time governments caught up. The transformative power of digital technology can disrupt traditional lacklustre public services, redefine regulation and make governments more efficient, open and accountable.

Crucially digital innovation puts the citizen back at the centre of the modern state in line with fundamental liberal and conservative principles.

Angus Taylor was elected to Federal parliament in 2013. In 2016 he was appointed Assistant Minister for Cities and Digital Transformation.

Series Editor: Nick Cater

Available from: www.connorcourt.com